Collins · family pet guide

D0345802

JINKINGS, Kathy

Aquarium fish

Kathy Jinkings

Kathy has kept and spawned many species of aquarium fish, both tropical and temperate. Currently specialising mainly in catfish, she is a regular contributor to both *Practical Fish Keeping* and *Aquarist and Pondkeeper* magazines, and an active member of several local and national fish societies.

ACKNOWLEDGEMENTS
With thanks to Dr David Sands for supplying many of the photographs, suggestions and support during the writing of this book.

Collins · family pet guides

AQUARIUM FISH

KATHY JINKINGS

First published in 2000 by
HarperCollins*Publishers*
77-85 Fulham Palace Road
Hammersmith
London W6 8JB

Collins is a registered trademark of
HarperCollins Publishers Limited.

The HarperCollins website address
is www.**fire**and**water**.com

09 08 07 06 05
9 8 7 6 5

Kathy Jinkings asserts the moral
right to be identified as the author
of this work.

A catalogue record of this book is
available from the British Library.

ISBN 0 00 413409 5

THIS BOOK WAS CREATED BY
SP Creative Design for
HarperCollins*Publishers* **Ltd**
EDITOR: Heather Thomas
DESIGN AND PRODUCTION:
Rolando Ugolini
PHOTOGRAPHY: All pictures are
supplied by Dr David Sands with
the following exceptions provided
by Max Gibbs: pages 1, 5, 10, 28,
38, 48, 50, 52, 57, 64, 65, 70, 74,
80, 88, 116
Kathy Jinkings: pages 108, 109

COLOUR REPRODUCTION BY
Colourscan, Singapore
PRINTED AND BOUND BY
Printing Express, Hong Kong

Contents

Introduction

Anyone who has ever found their eyes drawn to a tropical fish tank will be able to testify to the allure of watching the brightly coloured fish. As shoals of fish glide through plants, feed and court, they provide us with a relaxing and fascinating sight. To own such a display at home is not difficult and will give you many hours of pleasure.

Fish are one of the few pets that are suitable for nearly everyone; an aquarium will enhance a studio flat or a mansion equally, and is unlikely to cause complaints from the landlord or the neighbours. Even if you work irregular hours

or have little leisure time, have a limited budget, or are disabled, you can still enjoy the pleasures of fish keeping.

Although at first glance the fish may appear to be little more than ornaments, albeit beautiful ones, and not really in the class of 'pets' at all, you will soon realise that this is not the case. Each aquarium is a little slice of nature; the more you watch the fish the more you will appreciate their often complex behaviour and interaction with one another. Keeping fish is not only fun, but educational as well. The glass of your aquarium can be a window on to nature, where you can see at first hand and learn to understand the complexities of an underwater world that is usually hidden from human gaze.

The history of aquaria

We are lucky today in that modern technology has made aquarium keeping much easier. Electronic heaters and thermostats ensure that tanks are kept at the right temperature with no effort on the part of the fish keeper; modern filtration and aeration allow more fish to be kept in a healthy environment, and the variety of fish available is increasing almost daily. However, although fish keepers of the past did not have such advantages, the pleasures of fish keeping were such that people have been overcoming obstacles and enjoying aquarium fish for hundreds of years.

The first 'aquarium' fish was the goldfish. As long ago as 1596 in China, Chang Chi'en-te described the trials of doing water changes, of siphoning out fish droppings so that they would not pollute the water, and protecting his fish

Did you know?

The first public aquarium in the world was built in 1853 at the London Zoological Gardens. In it the first photograph of a living fish was taken by Count Montizon. Anyone who has tried to photograph speedy fish using modern photographic equipment will appreciate what a tremendous feat this was, using the technology of the day!

Above: *Goldfish were one of the first fish bred for keeping in early aquaria.*

from the heat of summer and also the cold of winter. Chang's 'aquarium' would have been a simple bowl rather than the glass structures we know now. This is why Chinese varieties of goldfish are bred to be beautiful when viewed from the top, whereas more modern species are bred to be appreciated from a side view.

Of course, goldfish aquaria are still attractive and popular, but there are now many other fish to choose from. The first of this vanguard was the Paradise fish. These fish are not so popular nowadays, although they are still kept by some aquarists, as they are very aggressive. In spite of their uncertain temper, the robust and hardy Paradise fish thrived in the care of the early aquarists. The first one arrived in France in 1868, imported by the French consul at Ningpo. These Chinese fish rapidly rewarded their keeper, Pierre Carbonnier, by spawning the following year!

In 1665, Samuel Pepys wrote in his well-known diary of keeping fish 'in a glass of water'; it seems likely that these were Paradise fish, which, unlike most fishes, could survive in such a small volume of water.

Types of aquaria

When most people think of aquariums, they have a mental picture of a tropical community – shoals of tiny brightly coloured fish darting around a jungle of lush foliage. However, many of us were introduced to the joys of fish keeping by owning a goldfish as a child, and goldfish aquaria are still deservedly popular. The wide range of varieties means that everyone will find a goldfish that appeals to them.

In addition to goldfish there are several other species of fish that can be kept in temperate (unheated) tanks, and these may be a good choice for someone worried about electricity and water being in proximity, for example in a child's bedroom. Without a heater, a tank can easily be set up with no electrical equipment in the water at all.

All the fishes and plants discussed in this book are freshwater. Many aquarists will later go on to keep marine or brackish aquaria, but it is recommended that you gain some experience with freshwater fish before attempting this, as many freshwater species are more forgiving of the errors of a learning aquarist!

Using this book

Because an aquarium is a living ecosystem, in which every part interacts with the other parts, it is impossible to tell you everything you need to know sequentially. For example, you may read the chapter on tanks and decide on everything you are going to buy, only to fall in love later with a species of fish that would prefer the aquarium to be set up differently. Read the book before making any decisions, and then you can refer back to the relevant chapters as you go through the process of actually buying and setting up your aquarium and fish.

CHAPTER ONE

Aquarium equipment

Obviously, before you can buy any fish, you will need to buy a tank to keep them in, and equip it so that the fish will have a healthy environment. Fish are very easy to keep; all you have to do is master the art of keeping water clean! You must buy all your equipment well in advance of your fish, but do bear in mind what sort of fish you hope to keep eventually. There is no point buying a 60-cm (2-ft) tank if you want to keep a group of goldfish which will soon need a bigger home.

What size aquarium?

The first thing to decide is where you will keep your tank. This will be governed by the space you have in which to put it. You might think that the easiest way is to start with a little tank. However, the bigger the tank, the easier it will be to keep healthy. After all, if a tiny fish dies in the corner of a big lake, nothing is affected too badly, but if the same fish dies in a teacup the water will very soon start to smell! Although you may be working to a strict budget, large second-hand tanks are often available cheaply through small ads in the local paper, or

Opposite: *Rainbow delta tail guppies*

through your local fish club. You may have to wait a while until the right one is available, but bargains are there to be found.

Tank design

When choosing a tank, you should be aware that some tanks you will see in the shops are designed to be visually attractive to humans but, unfortunately, not to fish. The water surface area needs to be as large as possible (so that oxygen can reach the water) and therefore your tank should be much longer or wider than it is tall. Avoid any of the 'high-tech' columnar tanks – these will not look nearly as attractive when they are full of dead fish that you cannot get out because you can't reach the bottom.

Siting the tank

The site you choose should be out of direct sunlight, and not above a radiator or other heat source; either of these will make it difficult for you to maintain a stable temperature. If you plan to

stand the tank on an existing piece of furniture, do consider how heavy water is; if the furniture collapses, you will not only have broken

Left: *A tank and stand supplied together not only look attractive, but the stand is built specially to support the great weight of water. Consider this if you plan to put your tank on an existing piece of furniture.*

Right: *When positioning your tank, remember that you not only need to be able to see it, but also to easily clean and work inside it.*

furniture but also fish and water all over the floor.

Aquarium shops sell many tanks complete with purpose-built stands, which are available in a wide range of different effects to complement your décor. If the tank is to go upstairs, consider whether the floor will hold it, and try to choose a position where the weight is distributed over several joists.

You will need to be able to remove water for water changes. If the tank is too low it will be hard to siphon water from it. If it is too high, you may find it difficult to reach into it for cleaning. A good height is at eye-level when you are sitting down.

What will the water in my tank weigh?

Calculate the volume of the tank by multiplying the length x width x height in centimetres. Each cubic centimetre of water weighs one gram. Divide the total by 1000 to get the number of kilograms.

Example:
90 cm (length) x 30 cm (width) x 38 cm (height) =
102,600 cubic cm/grams, or 102.6 cubic litres/kilograms.

Note: Don't forget that the rocks and decorations in the tank and the tank itself will add to the total weight.

CHAPTER
ONE

Filters

The filter is the most important piece of equipment you will buy. It is the job of the filter to remove the natural excretions of the fish from the water – without a working filter your fish will die, smothered in their own wastes. Never skimp on the size of the filter; if in doubt, choose a larger model rather than a smaller one. There are a wide variety of filters on the market, which can be bemusing to many first-time buyers. Some suitable different types of filter are described below.

Undergravel filter

An undergravel filter consists of a plate that sits underneath the gravel, connected to uplift tubes which stick up through the gravel. Water is sucked up the uplift tubes by either an air pump or by an electric powerhead pump. This creates a

Above: *This powerhead driving an undergravel filter provides a good water flow, oxygenating the gravel and turning over the* water surface to help dissolve as much oxygen as possible.

Which size powerhead for my undergravel?

Calculate the area of gravel by length x width (in centimetres) and divide by 204 to calculate the litres per hour.

To calculate the required gallons per hour, multiply the length x width (in inches) and divide by 144, then multiply by 60 (minutes in an hour).

An undergravel filter should pass a gallon a minute through each square foot of the aquarium gravel.

vacuum underneath the gravel, which means that water is sucked down through the gravel to fill it. As water passes through the gravel it is filtered biologically. Undergravel filters are good for small fish, which do not produce large volumes of waste, but need conscientious gravel cleaning to avoid them becoming clogged.

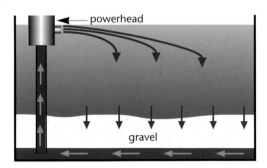

Left: *Undergravel filtration: The water is sucked down through the gravel and returned to the tank by the powerhead. As the water returns it disturbs the water surface, thereby increasing the oxygen content of the water.*

Internal power filter

This consists of a canister attached to a pump, which fits inside the aquarium. The pump moves water through the canister, which is filled with foam for biological filtration, or chemical filter media, such as carbon, for chemical filtration. This is good for

CHAPTER
ONE

Right: *Internal power filter:* *The water is drawn through the* inlets at the base of the canister, *and passes up through the sponge* *insert (visible in cutaway section).* *The water is then returned to the* *tank at the water surface, where* *the turbulence increases the* *oxygen level in the water.*

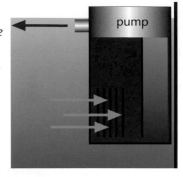

fish that produce lots of waste but it does take up space in your tank. The canister unclips so that you can wash the foam or change the filter media quickly and easily.

Which size of internal power filter?

Internal power filters are rated in gallons per hour, and yours should process all the water in the tank four times an hour. To calculate the number of gallons in the tank, multiply the length, height and width in centimetres. Divide the result by 1000 to get the number of litres, and divide this by 4.54 to get the number of gallons. Multiply the final result by 4 to find the gallons per hour you need for your filter.

Example:
90 cm (length) x 30 cm (width) x 38 cm (height) = 102600 cubic cm = 102.6 litres

102.6 litres/4.54 = 22.6 gallons

22.6 gallons 4 times an hour = 90.4 gph

Filter gallons per hour are measured with the canister empty rather than with the foam in, so when you buy yours go up to the next size rather than down a size. In the example above, a 100 gph filter would be suitable.

External power filter

This works in the same way as an internal power filter, but the pump and canister are located outside the tank. These filters are suitable for large messy fish, especially if the owner does not wish to have electrical equipment in the water but requires extra storage space outside the tank.

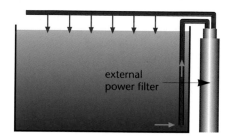

external
power filter

Left: *External power filter: the filter, located outside the tank, pumps water from the tank through the inlet pipe. The water circulates through the filter media inside the canister, then returns to the tank either by a simple pipe or a spray bar, as in this illustration.*

The ideal filter combination

For most aquaria a combination of an undergravel and an internal biological filter is a good choice. By using two devices, there is less risk of all the fish dying if one device fails or becomes clogged, as the second device continues to provide filtration. If you are out for large parts of the day, or want to go on holiday and leave your fish, such fail-safes are a good idea.

How filtration works

Filtration can be divided into three types: Mechanical, Biological and Chemical.

■ **Mechanical filtration** simply involves sieving out large particles of waste. In the internal and external power filters the waste is removed by washing or replacing the filter media. In an undergravel filter, the waste is still in the tank, trapped in the gravel, which must be cleaned regularly to avoid water fouling.

■ **Chemical filtration** involves placing special filter chemicals, such as carbon or zeolite, in the canisters of either internal or

CHAPTER
ONE

external filters. These catch invisible chemical pollutants, such as ammonia, by chemical reactions, and store the waste within the media. It is very important that the media be replaced regularly in accordance with the instructions, or it may stop working.

■ **Biological filtration** involves encouraging natural bacteria to live in a filter medium with a large surface area – a sponge inside the power filters, or the surfaces of the stones in the gravel. One sort of bacteria eats ammonia, which fish excrete. Like everything that eats, bacteria also excrete, but they excrete a different chemical – nitrite – which is still poisonous to fish. Fortunately, however, a second type of bacteria eats nitrite and excretes nitrate, which is not very toxic to fish. Eventually the aquarist removes the nitrate build-up during water changes. For the bacteria to survive in large numbers they need oxygen, so fresh water must be circulated continuously to keep the bacteria healthy.

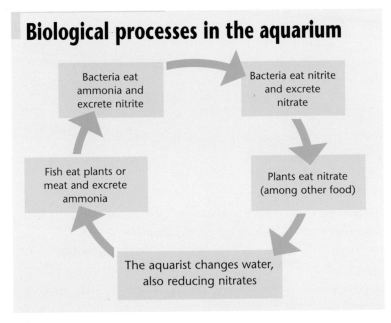

Biological processes in the aquarium

Bacteria eat ammonia and excrete nitrite

Bacteria eat nitrite and excrete nitrate

Plants eat nitrate (among other food)

The aquarist changes water, also reducing nitrates

Fish eat plants or meat and excrete ammonia

Heating the water

For most tropical fish you will need to heat the water to between 22°C and 25°C (72–78°F). All the tropical fish described in this book will thrive at these temperatures, although if you buy a different species be sure to find out as much as you can about it first, to make sure it is suitable for your tank.

Although modern heaters and thermostats are very reliable, it is better to buy two smaller heaters and position one at each end of the tank. This results in more even heating of the water, and if one thermostat breaks the remaining heater is unlikely to have enough strength to boil your fish.

Heaters come in a variety of types; the easiest to use are those with a temperature scale as part of the heater (rather than just plus or minus), and which can be completely submersed in water.

Note: Temperate fish do not need a heater in the aquarium (see pages 44–50).

Which size heater?

You should allow one watt per litre of water.

Example:
90 cm (length) x 30 cm (width) x 38 cm (height) = 102,600 cubic cm = 102.6 cubic litres

This tank would need a single 100-watt heater or, better still, two 50-watt heaters.

If your house is centrally heated and usually warm (even at night) you can choose the next size down from the heater calculation, but if your house is sometimes very cold you should choose the next size up.

CHAPTER
ONE

Lighting

Most tank hoods have room to fit one fluorescent light. If you want to specialize in interesting plants you will need to increase this, but for a beginner's tank with a few hardy plants you won't need more lighting than this. You will need a fluorescent tube of a length suitable to fit the tank, plus a starter unit for that size of bulb. Any starter unit cannot be used with any bulb, so ask for advice if you are not sure.

Buying accessories

In addition to the essential equipment so far described, you will need to buy a few extra things to make your aquarium look attractive and make life easier for you.

Gravel
If you have chosen to have an undergravel filter, gravel is essential, and you must buy enough of it to cover the tank bottom to a

Above: *Common goldfish are not as ornate as their fancy cousins, but still make a fine aquarium display.*

depth of 5–7.5 cm (2–3 in). If you are not using an undergravel, then the gravel (or substrate) is simply to make the tank look nice, and you do not need as much. Gravel is available in many colours, from 'natural' to fluorescent pink, so you can choose a colour depending on your tastes. Consider the fish that you prefer; fish such as neon tetras will look best with a dark substrate, but if you like black fish you will need a lighter colour if you ever want to see them. Always buy gravel from the aquarium shop; stones collected from a building site or beach may contain pollutants, or there may be metal ores in the stones. Either of these will result in your fish dying for no apparent cause. It is better to be safe than sorry.

Thermometer

You will need a thermometer to check that your tank is at the correct temperature. These are inexpensive and available in various types. The most reliable are those that go inside the tank, and they are usually attached to the side by a rubber suction cup. Thermometers stuck on the outside glass are more convenient but do not report the temperature inside the tank as accurately.

Water tests

It is good practice to perform various tests on the tank water regularly so that you can spot any problems to prevent the fish getting sick. Therefore before you even start keeping fish, you should test your tap water to find out its pH and hardness. Although these can be altered, it is much simpler to choose fish that will thrive in the tap water as it is. Once you have started stocking the tank, you will need to test the water regularly for ammonia and nitrite, especially during the first crucial days when the bacteria are colonizing the biological filters.

Water tests are available in a number of different forms, including tablets or drops that you mix with water in a test tube, or dip-in strips with special indicator coatings. All the tests involve comparing the resulting colours with those printed on a chart.

Look at the chart before you buy the test; even people who are not colour-blind sometimes have difficulty distinguishing between some of the colours. If all the colours on a particular test chart appear to be the same, try looking at a card from a different manufacturer or type of test. If you are completely unable to distinguish the colours on any of the tests, you may want to consider a digital test meter which will give you a reading that does not rely on colour comparison. These are, however, quite expensive.

Dechlorinator

The water companies produce tap water to be safe for humans to drink. This is not the same as safe for fish to live in. So that human diseases cannot flourish in the water, it is treated with chlorine. This is harmless to people but very dangerous for fish. Any tap water that you put in your tank (including the first time you fill it) must have the chlorine removed. This is not difficult; you just buy a bottle of dechlorinator and add the amount indicated on the bottle for the amount of water you are treating.

Filter starter

This is a bottle of the bacteria that is required to colonize the biological filter. Filter starter is an optional extra; the filter will be

Backdrop

This is an optional extra, purely for your visual appreciation. Aquarium shops sell a range of pictures for use as backdrops, ranging from natural scenes to the more unlikely. If you are working to a budget, you could try sticking a black plastic bag to the back of the tank (outside, not inside!) which can be very effective. Mirror tiles can also look impressive.

Above: *Natural bogwood provides a decoration that looks both natural and interesting as well as providing a dietary supplement for Loricariid catfish, such as this whiptail.*

colonized anyway eventually. However, you can speed up the process and help your aquarium get started with some of this.

Electric extension block

It is easy to forget when making all the arrangements that power filters, lights and heaters all need to be plugged in. It is possible to buy cable tidies to wire in all your devices, but this makes life complicated if you want to change a unit when it breaks (which invariably happens when you are on your way out to work, or have got home late). Count the number of sockets near your tank and, if necessary, get a four-way extension.

Electricity trip switch

Although modern electrical equipment is very safe, if you have any equipment inside the tank in the water, such as heaters or power filters, it is sensible to connect them to a trip switch which can plug into the wall socket. The extension block or device plugs into the trip switch. If an electrical fault occurs, the trip switch will cut off all the electricity, thereby ensuring that you do not get a nasty shock.

Electric timer

If you work irregular hours, you can put the aquarium lighting on an electric timer. This will ensure that the lights come on and go off at predefined times; the fish can become stressed if they have a week of darkness, a few days of normal lighting, and then a week of lights on. The plants will almost certainly not survive such treatment, as they depend on light to be able to feed.

Hoses and buckets

You will have to change some of the water in the tank regularly, as well as filling it up initially. It is advisable to have a special siphon hose and bucket for the tank. Making the bleach bucket serve a dual purpose can lead to very unpleasant surprises, even if you think you have washed it out properly. If you already have a hose and bucket you can reserve for this task, and are sure they

Equipment checklist

Essential items:	Optional items:
■ Tank	■ Tank decorations
■ Filter	■ Backdrop
■ Heater for tropical fish	■ Filter starter
■ Light bulb	■ Electric socket expansion block
■ Starter gravel	
■ Thermometer	■ Electricity trip switch
■ Water tests for pH, hardness, ammonia and nitrite	■ Electric timer for the lights
	■ Hose and bucket
■ Dechlorinator	

are clean, wash them again a few times to be on the safe side and keep them for aquarium use only.

Decorations

A wide range of tank decorations are available from aquarium shops, ranging from natural rocks and bogwood pieces in convoluted shapes to preformed caves and fake tree-trunks. A child might enjoy a tank decorated with some of the many fluorescent skulls, sunken ships and other ornaments, or one of those powered by an air pump with a moving diver or treasure chest. The fish will not mind any of these, so you are limited only by your own tastes. If you plan to include some of the algae-eating loricariids, then have at least a small piece of bogwood – they enjoy chewing on this. New bogwood often leaches tannin into the water. If you have softwater fish they will appreciate this, but hardwater species, such as guppies, would be happier without it. Soaking the bogwood for a few weeks before placing it in the tank can mitigate this effect. Some woods on sale, such as mopani, do not leach tannins but are slightly more expensive.

Above: *A variety of stones are available from your aquarium shop, and are guaranteed safe for use in your tank.*

Above: *These plastic pipes have been covered with gravel to make them more attractive, and will be popular hiding places for catfish and loaches.*

Right: *The natural nooks and crannies of bogwood make a good shelter for fish as well as being decorative.*

▌ Putting it all together

When you have your equipment, you need to set it all up together to run for a while before the fish arrive. This gives you a period of time in order to check that everything is working as it should.

Setting up the tank

1 Wash out the tank – it may have dust or other dirt in it.

2 Put the tank in its correct position – be sure it is right before you fill it with water. Even a small full tank is very heavy, and you will not be able to move it without emptying it again. If your tank is the type where the whole bottom surface is in contact with the stand, then put down some polystyrene tiles or a piece of carpet, cut to the same size as the tank. Once the weight of water is pressing down on it, a piece of grit so small you didn't notice it will be big enough to stress and crack the tank.

3 If you are using an undergravel, cut the plates to size if needed and assemble it with the uplift tubes and the powerhead (not switched on) in the aquarium. You may need to cut the uplift tubes shorter to make it all fit. Once the undergravel fits well, remove the powerhead and leave the plate and fitted uplift tubes.

4 Wash the gravel thoroughly until the water runs clear. Even if it claims to be pre-washed, wash it again. You will be surprised at the amount of dirt and dust that washes away which would have ended up in your tank.

5 Spread the gravel over the filter plate evenly, making sure that the areas behind the uplift tube and in the corners are equally well covered. Some books may advise you to make it deeper at the back, but gravity and the fish will soon disabuse you of this idea once the tank is set up and running.

6 Place a saucer on the gravel, and pour the water on to the saucer (avoiding knocking all your carefully spread gravel out of the way) until the tank is half-full.

7 Position the heater, powerhead and internal filter in the tank. Add some decorations to make the tank look attractive. You can then fill the tank up fully.

8 Add dechlorinator to the water, as instructed on the bottle.

9 If you used cold water, wait until it reaches room temperature and then switch on all the electrical equipment and add the thermometer. Powerheads and power filters should be issuing a steady stream of water, and after a day the thermometer should show that the water has reached the correct temperature. You may need to adjust the heater(s) a few times to get this right. When the tank is first set up, oxygen will bubble out of the water and accumulate as a myriad of tiny bubbles on the sides of the tank. This is perfectly normal and nothing to worry about.

10 After a few days, if all is well, you can go and buy your first fish.

Below: *Plants can be used to great effect in making the aquarium a fitting backdrop to the colourful fish.*

CHAPTER TWO

Understanding aquarium fish

You will be more successful and derive more pleasure from your finny charges if you understand a little about how they are put together and think. Over time, watching your fish will teach you even more about them.

▌ Breathing

There are advantages and disadvantages to living in water. Water is about 1,000 times as dense as air, and contains far less oxygen. For many fish, the oxygen content of the water, and their ability to breathe it, makes the difference between life and death.

Fishes get oxygen by passing the water over their gills. The gills are blood-rich filaments that are kept out of harm's way behind the operculum, or gill cover. As oxygen in the water passes over the gills, it passes through into the blood, which is continuously flowing through the gills. If there is not enough oxygen in the water, the fish will breathe very fast and appear to be panting. They may hang around at the surface of the water, trying to breathe from the atmosphere. If your aquarium is overstocked with fish this may happen. Oxygen enters the

■ **Opposite:** *Tiger barbs*

Air breathers

Many fish are able to breathe air as well, especially those that come from areas where the water may become stagnant. Paradise fish, the first tropical fish to be kept, come into this category, which is how they managed to survive in Samuel Pepys' glass of water. Others, such as many of the catfish, are able to swallow air and absorb the oxygen in the intestine. When the oxygen levels fall, air breathers head for the surface and take in air, and will survive when other fish have died. Baby fish are not always so good at this as adults, and may die in oxygen-depleted water.

water by being dissolved at the water surface, so the more turbulent the water is at the surface the more oxygen will be dissolved. Filters perform this function as an 'extra' advantage, by disturbing the water surface as the water returns to the tank from the pumps. However, if the fish are dependent on this extra oxygen and the filter becomes clogged or breaks, then the oxygen will deplete rapidly and the fish will start to suffocate.

Fish can also experience breathing difficulties if the gills are damaged. This can occur if they are subjected to a poison such as chlorine. If you do not dechlorinate the new water during water changes, the fish may appear to be alright, but might have suffered damage to their gills. It will take very little depletion of the oxygen in the water for such fish to start to show signs of distress, and they may die.

Living with water

Fish are completely and utterly dependent on the water in which they live. They breathe it, drink it and are continually bathed in it. It is not surprising, therefore, that if the water is polluted they will become unhappy. If the water is seriously foul, of course, they will simply die. However, if the water contains just a little bit too much ammonia (which is any at all) or poisons enter (from undechlorinated tap water, or air fresheners sprayed too close, or a touch of fly spray) it may not be enough to kill them but just enough to make life difficult. Bad water may irritate their skins, causing permanent itching; it may also damage the gills, meaning that they have to work for every breath. Although such things may not kill the fish outright, the individuals in such a tank will suffer continually from minor ailments, which will recur as soon as they have been treated. In such circumstances, continually dosing the fish with remedies will have no real effect. However, if given some clean healthy water the disease outbreaks will stop.

Parts of a fish

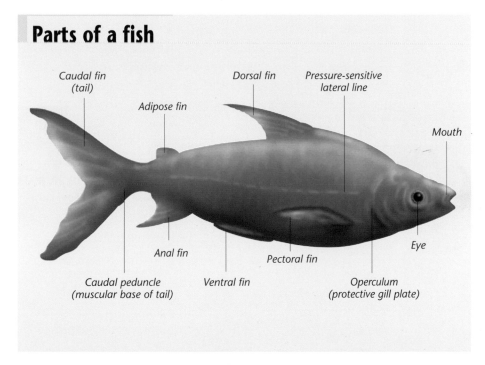

Caudal fin (tail)

Adipose fin

Dorsal fin

Pressure-sensitive lateral line

Mouth

Eye

Anal fin

Pectoral fin

Caudal peduncle (muscular base of tail)

Ventral fin

Operculum (protective gill plate)

CHAPTER
TWO

Energy requirements

One of the advantages of living in dense water is the fact that the water supports the fish's body. If you relax completely you will fall over, but a relaxed fish stays in the same place. They only need to use energy to actually move. For this reason it is easy for a beginner to overfeed fish. To give fish a hearty meal on the same scale as you would a human, dog or cat would be to give it far too much food. The extra food will either remain uneaten or be swallowed and excreted with no nutrition taken out by the fish. This waste will quickly rot, overloading the filters and polluting the tank water. If the water becomes foul, the fish will die.

Feeling secure

Provided they have enough air and food and are not living in foul water, happiness, for a fish, is very simple to achieve. Fish are happy if they believe that, at any given moment, they are not about to be eaten by another fish. The fact of whether or not there is another fish in the tank that might eat them is irrelevant; fish in nature are never too confident about what might at that very moment be heading upstream towards them. Fishes have developed a number of ways of dealing with this prospect of imminent death.

Left: *These shoaling clown loaches are unhappy if kept without the company of others of their kind.*

Shoaling fish

Some fish are shoaling – they live in large groups of their own kind. When a predator finds a shoal, the large numbers of fish milling around may confuse it, and furthermore the odds of any particular individual being eaten fall depending on the number of alternative snacks it is shoaling with. If you keep a shoaling fish alone, it will be sad and stressed – not because it is lonely, as a human would be, but because it believes it is in danger of becoming another fish's dinner.

Above: *Solitary tiger barbs become unpleasant bullies. Kept in a group, they are occupied with one another.*

Timid and reclusive fish

Other fish rely on being able to blend into the background, or hide in plants or caves. You can stress these fish by keeping them in a tank where there is nowhere for them to hide, or on a gravel that makes them stand out. If you have a community tank, it is best to keep species of similar sizes. You may know that the gentle giant you have just added won't hurt the little fish, but they don't know that, and will live short, terrified lives.

Right: *This rainbow fish feels safer and looks its best with some plants that it could hide behind.*

CHAPTER
TWO

> **Above:** *Tetras often come from blackwater streams and will feel exposed and nervous in bright tanks.*

Dominant and aggressive fish

Some species of fish are bullies and will harass other fish, even bigger ones. A timid fish which is unable to get away from another continually nipping at its fins and chasing it will also be very stressed. A happy community contains fish that are of roughly the same temperament. With some fish that are prone to aggression, it is best to keep large groups. The theory behind this is that although the dominant fish will not become any less nasty, they will have lots of choices to vent their spite on. Thus it is not one poor individual who continually bears the brunt of the attacks alone. Removing the main offender will not help, as the next fish in the 'pecking order' will simply assume the top spot.

Territorial fish

Dwarf gouramis, *Colisa lalia*, are both shoaling and territorial. If there are lots of them in a tank, they will swim together, but if there are only a few they will try to establish territories. If there is not quite enough room for this, some individuals will be harassed to death to make room!

If you want to keep these fish, it is best to keep a single male, which will not bother attacking fishes of other species, as he only feels his territory threatened by other male dwarf gouramis.

▌ A home to go to

Some species are territorial and will require a small part of the aquarium to call their own. This is usually true of those fish that guard their eggs, and need to establish a safe place for the spawning. While you might think a 1-m (3-ft) tank is plenty big enough, a fish from a vast lake cannot be expected to see it in the same light. You can help them create individual territories by using the décor and tank ornaments to break up the line of sight, so that each fish in its own territory cannot see the one in the territory next door. Some fish will become stressed by other fish encroaching on their territory, but more aggressive species will regard offence as the best form of defence and launch full-out, often fatal, attacks on the perceived invaders.

Species that guard their eggs often offer other pitfalls for the aquarist. While their keeper might assume that a male and female pair will be idyllically happy and that nature will take its course, the path of true love is often not smooth in the fishy

▌ **Right:** *This sheepshead acara is guarding its eggs, and may become aggressive if the other fish cannot keep out of its way.*

Right: *These large cichlids are territorial, and fights result if one feels that another is coming too close.*

world. In many species, if a female approaches a male's territory, he assumes it is because she wants to spawn. If she is there simply because there is nowhere else for her to go, fatal disagreements are likely to erupt. Assuming that the female is in fact looking for a husband and that the happy couple manage to pair up and produce some eggs, the proud father may suddenly realise that his wife is now hungry after all that effort. Of course, the nearest snack available is fish eggs! For this reason males often become very aggressive towards their partners after spawning, and may kill the female

if she is unable to leave the area. As with ordinary territoriality, the aquarist can counteract this antisocial behaviour by providing lots of décor that breaks up the line of sight so that the female can avoid the male during the times she is surplus to requirements (which is most of the time).

Left: *This cichlid is making a threat display to an intruder.*

Dying of stress

While a stressed human might have a nervous breakdown, a stressed fish will almost certainly die. It will not feed properly, being too scared to come into the open for food. Also, the stress weakens the immune systems, so that it falls prey to diseases, such as white spot and fungus. Many aquarists continually treat their fish, unable to understand why disease is perpetually breaking out in the tank rather than looking at the causes of the fish being too weak to withstand the diseases in the first place. Not unreasonably, fish are also badly stressed by polluted water.

Symptoms of stress

You can tell that your fish are stressed if they try to jam themselves into corners, dart about frantically, or change colour. When they are upset, fish will turn very dark or very pale, and this warning sign should be noticed and dealt with by the responsible aquarist. In extreme stress, fish may even jump out of the water, and die by either escaping the tank altogether or banging themselves on the cover glass.

By watching your fish you will learn their normal behaviour patterns and colours, and quickly be able to see if they are behaving abnormally or are coloured differently. Fish rarely change their behaviour patterns just because they fancy a change; if a normally active fish suddenly starts hiding or a greedy fish stops feeding, there will certainly be a cause behind the effect.

Above: *This sad fish is suffering acute stress with discolouration and is lying on the bottom of the tank instead of swimming.*

CHAPTER THREE

Which fish?

The beauty of different aquarium fishes is definitely in the eye of the beholder. While one aquarist might be desperate to have a community tank of tetras, another may aspire to a tank of fancy goldfish, or perhaps a tank based on Asian gouramis and loaches. Still another will see a small brown fish in a shop and fall in love with it, despite the fact that it looks totally uninteresting to all his friends and relations.

P rovided that the object of your admiration grows to a size you can accommodate, then if you want it enough you will almost certainly buy it. However, you can make sure that your joy at your new purchase does not end in tears, finding it dead in the morning, by reading everything you can about it before giving it a home. Some fishes will require specialized care: for instance, some are aggressive carnivores that require a tank on their own and endless hours of chopping up bits of meat.

Believe the worst of what you read: if a fish is reported to be a one-metre-long (3-ft) predator there is no chance that yours will turn out to be a 15-cm (6-in) pussycat. It will eat all the other fish in the tank, and it will either cost

Did you know?

It is often rumoured that fishes will grow to the size of the tank they are in and then stop. This is absolutely true. The stopping process is also known as death, and the fish will indeed grow no more afterwards.

■ **Opposite:** *Red tailed catfish*

CHAPTER
THREE

you a lot of money rehoming it or it will die for lack of space. Out of the 10,000 or so fishes that have been seen at one time or another in aquarists' tanks, there are plenty that will fit into a community aquarium happily. To build a community around your desired fish, find out all you can about it and then choose tankmates of a similar size, temperament and preferences – there is no point surrounding your prize guppies with a gang of rambunctious fin-nipping barbs.

▌ How many fish?

The amount of oxygen that can be dissolved in water varies with the temperature. You can keep more fish in a tropical, heated aquarium than in an unheated temperate aquarium. Since oxygen is absorbed into the water from the surface, the calculation to work out how many fish you can keep is based

Above: *Goldfish come in many forms and colours, and remain the first choice of many aquarists.*

Natural-born killers

Although there are a few species which are exclusively vegetarian, most fish will see anything that fits into their mouths as food. Small fish like Neon tetras can easily end up as an appetizer for a larger tank mate, and new fry will be hoovered up with avidity, often by their own parents!

Above: *It may not look that pretty, and it is a voracious predator, but even this leaf fish is a fascinating creature that has its fans among aquarists.*

Right: *Always find out about fish before you buy them – this piranha would wreak havoc in a community aquarium tank.*

Above: *This beautiful Siamese fighter is easily bullied by fin-nippers and will be reduced to rags in all but the quietest aquaria.*

on the surface area, not the size of the tank. A tall tank with only a small surface area will home less fish than one of the same capacity that is low, long and wide.

Working out the surface area

You can find the surface area of a rectangular tank by multiplying the length and width to give you the total area. To work out the number of centimetres of fish you can keep in a tropical aquarium divide by 30; or by 60 to give you the number of centimetres of fish you can keep in a temperate aquarium.

Example:

90 cm (long) x 30 cm (wide) = 2700 square centimetres surface area. 2700 divided by 30 = 90 centimetres of tropical fish; or 2700 divided by 60 = 45 centimetres of temperate fish.

The temperate golden minnow can reach 10 cm, so you could keep four fish in this tank, along with 5 cm of another smaller species.

To calculate the number of inches of fish you can keep, divide the surface area (in square inches) by 12 for tropical fish; 24 for temperate fish.

This calculation gives you some good guidelines. However, if you are keeping big fish, then allow more space. Although a fancy goldfish, at 20 cm (8 in), is only twice as long as a golden minnow, it takes only a quick glance to realise that its body mass is many times greater. It will excrete far more than two minnows, and will need more oxygen. For large fish, allow at least 36 inches of surface area per inch of fish – the tank described above will really only suit one fully-grown goldfish! It is better to err on the side of caution than to mistakenly overstock your tank and find all your fish dead.

Above: *Redtails are often sold as cute 'kittens' but rapidly grow to metre-long catfish!*

CHAPTER
THREE

TEMPERATE SPECIES

Goldfish *(Carassius auratus auratus)*

Fish size comparisons

All fish 'fact panels' have a fish's size icon that compares it to the size of one of the largest fish in this book – the goldfish.

Goldfish facts
- **Length:** 20 cm (8 in) plus
- **Aquarium size:** 1 m (3 ft)
- **Staple diet:** goldfish flake or pellets
- **Swims:** midwater or top ■ **Spawning:** egg scatterers

├─ GOLDFISH: 20 CM (8 IN) ─┤

■ **Background:** Goldfish are tough and resilient fish, ideal for a beginner, but be warned that they can grow quite large, usually up to around 20 cm (8 in) in the aquarium, possibly even bigger. Goldfish are the earliest fish ever to have been kept indoors for their beauty, and are still just as popular today. Goldfish types can be roughly divided into two forms:

■ The long-bodied 'ancestral' types, such as the common goldfish and comets.

■ The round-bodied 'fancy' goldfish.

■ **Appearance:** Fancy goldfish varieties have a wide range of shapes, fins and colours, and the tail is often divided into two, rather than the single tail fin of the common fish. Often crossbreeds will be seen in aquarium shops – a nymph is a fish that has a round-bodied shape but only a single tail fin. These are looked down on by goldfish breeders, but they can still be attractive and fun to keep in a home aquarium.

■ **Community suitability:** It is unwise to mix long- and round-bodied goldfish in the same aquarium, as the round body shape is less streamlined and these are slow-swimming fish. Being forced to compete for food and swimming space with the darting forms of comets can result in the slower fish becoming stressed, getting less to eat, and even being accidentally knocked about in the passage

Above: *In spite of the development of the fancy variety of goldfish, the common goldfish is still very popular.*

of their faster cousins. A gentle output from the filter is desirable for goldfish; if an internal power filter is used, turn it to face across the aquarium, rather than lengthways. This will make it easier for the fish to stay out of the current. All varieties of goldfish are generally peaceful, and can make a stunning aquarium display.

Varieties of fancy goldfish

■ **Moor:** This is a beautiful velvety black fish, with protruding eyes and a long tail fin.

■ **Oranda:** The most noticeable characteristic of the oranda is the 'wen', an ornate growth on the top and sides of the head. In addition to this, they have long trailing fins, and occur in many colours – red, white, grey, chocolate and white. The tancho oranda is particularly attractive, being white with a red wen.

■ **Ranchu:** This has a similar head growth and range of colours to the oranda, but differs from it in having a shorter and neater tail and no dorsal fin.

CHAPTER
THREE

■ **Bubble-eye:** This fish takes its name from the large fluid-filled sacs which appear underneath the eye, forcing it to look upwards. These need special care and avoidance of sharp objects in the aquarium, to prevent the delicate bubbles from being damaged.

❖ *Ranchu goldfish*

■ **Celestial:** This fish also gazes up towards the sky, but the eyes simply turn up, rather than having the filled sac of the bubble-eye. The upward gaze is much more pronounced.

■ **Fantail:** One of the most popular fancy goldfish, which occurs in a wide range of colours, the fantail simply has long trailing fins and a trailing fan-shaped tail.

❖ *Chocolate oranda*

Golden minnow *(Pimephales promelas)*

Golden minnow facts
- **Length:** 7.5–10 cm (3–4 in)
- **Aquarium size:** 1 m (3 ft)
- **Staple diet:** goldfish flake
- **Swims:** midwater or top ■ **Spawning:** eggs, parental care

■ **Background:** The golden, or rosy, minnow is an aquarium variation of a brown American fish. They are attractive and energetic shoaling fish, never happier than when they are playing in the outflow from a filter. These are easy to spawn in the aquarium and, unusually among coldwater aquarium fish, the eggs are laid in a cave where the male guards them until

❖ *Female golden minnow*

hatching. For this reason they will be happiest in an aquarium where there is suitable décor for them to establish their small spawning territories. The male minnow grows a fleshy pad on top of his head, making him easy to sex. This gives rise to the American common name of fathead minnow.

Left: *This mature male golden minnow shows the thick pad of flesh on the head that gives rise to its other common name, 'fathead minnow'.*

CHAPTER
THREE

White cloud mountain minnow
(Tanichthys albonubes)

White cloud minnow facts
- *Length:* 2.5–4 cm (1–1¾ in)
- *Aquarium size:* 60 cm (2 ft)
- *Staple diet:* coldwater or tropical flake
- *Swims:* midwater or top ▪ *Spawning:* egg scatterers

▪ *Background:* The white cloud minnow hails from the mountains of China, where it inhabits streams. In the aquarium, it prefers lower room temperatures to tropical ones, but is nonetheless usually found in the tropical section of fish shops rather than among the coldwater fish.

▪ *Appearance:* These tiny minnows are very attractive with a brilliant red and cream line running along the brown body, red fins and a cream underside. This beauty leads to them being known as the 'poor man's neon', and although neon tetras are now a lot cheaper than they were, the mountain minnow remains deservedly popular in its own right.

▪ *Community suitability:* Like all minnows, they prefer to be kept in a small shoal and with a reasonable water current. Because of their small size, these are not good tankmates for goldfish.

❖ *White cloud mountain minnow*

▌ **Bitterling** *(Rhodeus sericeus)*

Bitterling facts
- *Length:* 10 cm (4 in)
- *Aquarium size:* 60 cm (2 ft)
- *Staple diet:* coldwater or tropical flake
- *Swims:* midwater or top ■ *Spawning:* eggs, parental care

■ *Appearance:* This is a peaceful fish which is often passed by in the shop as its best colours are only seen when it is in breeding condition. Fortunately, all that is required to bring the fish into such condition is the presence of a swan mussel (which is available from an aquarium shop), and the male becomes spectacular with rainbow hues of metallic blue and red on the silver background. No-one seeing a tank of plain grey fish in the shop would guess that this is one of the most beautiful of all temperate species.

■ *Community suitability and breeding:* These fish can be kept as a small group or as a pair, and are active and interesting. Even if no mussel is provided, they will still entertain by chasing through the tank, but if they are given a mussel the courtship procedure starts. The male and female bump into the mussel until it is desensitized and no longer snaps shut when approached. Once this has happened, the female extends a long grey ovipositor (which is often visible for several days before and after spawning) and inserts her eggs into the mussel. The male produces his sperm, which is drawn into the mussel after the eggs by the mussel's own intake of water for feeding. Within the mussel, the eggs hatch and the fry grow, until they are ready to leave the safety of the mussel shell and venture into the aquarium. Unfortunately, mussels are quite difficult to keep in aquaria, and therefore are best kept outside in a pond and brought in for aquarium duty in rotation.

CHAPTER
THREE

Above: *A pair of Chinese bitterlings court above a swan mussel which is used as part of the bitterling's mating ritual.*

Various species of bitterling occur throughout Europe and Asia, and different ones may occasionally show up in aquarium shops. All have very similar requirements. If you are planning to keep bitterling in Britain, you will have to get a licence from the Ministry of Agriculture, Fisheries and Food. The licence is completely free, and the requirement is for the protection of our own native fishes, so you should not let this deter you from keeping such interesting fish.

TROPICAL SPECIES

Guppy *(Poecilia reticulata)*

Guppy facts
- **Length:** female 6 cm (2½ in);
  male 4 cm (1¾ in)
- **Aquarium size:** 60 cm (2 ft) **pH:** 7–8
- **Staple diet:** tropical flake
- **Swims:** midwater or top **Spawning:** livebearer

Nearly everyone is familiar with the popular guppy. These little fish are so resilient that breeding colonies have become established across the world, either by aquarists releasing specimens or deliberately as a form of mosquito control. There is even a group of these prolific fish thriving in an English river, in a heated power station outflow. The guppy in our aquariums is considerably

Below: *The female guppy, although larger than the male, is not so brightly coloured.*

CHAPTER
THREE

Above: *This male rainbow delta tail guppy shows the spectacularly coloured fins for which they are noted.*

different from its wild cousin. Wild guppies, although pretty, are smaller and do not exhibit the amazing range of gorgeous colours and different tail shapes that our domestic fish show.

Guppies prefer hard water, and would be unhappy if kept in a pH below 7 (neutral). Apart from this, they are unfussy fish that will thrive and breed, and there is a guppy to suit everyone. Greens, blues, reds, yellows and even black, single colours and patterns, and tails from the long trailing beauty of the veiltail to the neat attraction of the round cofertail provide an array to suit every taste.

Guppy males are smaller and more brightly coloured than the females, so the temptation is to own lots of males and only a few females. However, this is unfair on the fish as the males will become worn out competing with each other and the few females will be in such demand that they will be constantly harassed. It is better to keep two females to each male. A well-planted aquarium will show off the guppies' colours against the plants and provide the necessary cover for the females to find a little peace and quiet while giving birth.

Platy *(Xiphophorus maculatus)*

Platy facts
- **Length:** female 6 cm (2½ in); male 2.5 cm (1 in)
- **Aquarium size:** 60 cm (2 ft) ■ **pH:** 7–8
- **Staple diet:** tropical flake
- **Swims:** midwater or top ■ **Spawning:** livebearer

Platies are also livebearers but have a number of advantages over guppies. Although the colours are not usually as bright or as varied, they are still available in a wide choice of varieties and the females are also brightly coloured, unlike the duller guppy females. Platy tails are usually short and compact, enabling the pleasantly plump little fish to cope with companions that might find the lure of trailing guppy tails too much to resist a quick nip. Their care is the same as for the guppy, and these attractive fish put on a very good show. If you can't make up your mind, guppies and platies get along quite well together in the aquarium and are from separate families so hybridization is unlikely.

❖ *Platy*

▌Swordtail *(Xiphophorus hellerii)*

Swordtail facts

■ *Length:* female 12.5 cm (5 in);
   male 10 cm (4 in)
■ *Aquarium size:* 1 m (3 ft)   ■ *pH:* 7–8
■ *Staple diet:* tropical flake
■ *Swims:* midwater or top   ■ *Spawning:* livebearer

Swordtails are ideal livebearers for the larger aquarium, growing to a much larger size than the small guppies and platies. They are equally easy to keep and breed, and although there are not as many colour varieties they are still attractive fish. The major enhancement of the swordtail is in the male's sword, a long extension to the tail. This has not been created domestically, but is a feature of the wild fish as well.

Other than the sword, the fins are small and neat. Some

▌**Above:** *This male swordtail shows a well-developed 'sword', a
natural modification to his tail.*

long-fin swordtails have been bred, but these often have difficulty reproducing due to malformation of the gonopodium (the male's specially modified anal fin which is used to inseminate the female) and are best avoided by the beginner.

Swordtails should not be kept in the same aquarium as platies, as they are prone to hybridization. Swordtails are peaceful towards other aquarium inhabitants, but males can be very quarrelsome between themselves. Keeping a trio of a male and two females should avoid any trouble developing.

Glowlight tetra *(Hemigrammus erythrozonus)*

Glowlight facts
- **Length:** 4 cm (1¾ in)
- **Aquarium size:** 60 cm (2 ft) ■ **pH:** 6–7.5
- **Staple diet:** tropical flake
- **Swims:** midwater ■ **Spawning:** egg layers

The glowlight tetra will disappear into obscurity in a bright tank, but in a dark tank, with lots of plants or a black gravel, they will live up to their name and glow like beacons. These peaceful fish are a pale brown, but their glow comes from the iridescent red stripe down the side that appears to shine as though lit from within. They are shoaling fish that should always be kept in a group of six or so.

❖ Glowlight tetra

CHAPTER
THREE

Neon tetra *(Paracheirodon innesi)* and
Cardinal tetra *(Paracheirodon axelrodi)*

Neon tetra facts
- *Length:* 2.5 cm (1 in)
- *Aquarium size:* 60 cm (2 ft) ■ *pH:* 6–8
- *Staple diet:* tropical flake
- *Swims:* midwater ■ *Spawning:* egg layers

Cardinal tetra facts
- *Length:* 5 cm (2 in)
- *Aquarium size:* 60 cm (2 ft) ■ *pH:* 7–8
- *Staple diet:* tropical flake
- *Swims:* midwater ■ *Spawning:* egg layers

These related tetras are very similar in appearance, both featuring a bright blue 'neon' stripe down the side. The cardinal tetra is completely red below the stripe, whereas the neon is only red towards the back.

In the aquarium, both species are peaceful and shoaling and dislike bright lights. In a dark aquarium, they show their colours to best effect, gleaming like lights as they flash around the tank.

❖ *Cardinal tetras*

The neon is slightly hardier and is more tolerant than the cardinal, and reaches a slightly smaller size. In practice, both neons and cardinals can be acclimatized to harder water, and if you buy yours from a local shop there should be no problem in keeping them in your tap water. Both fish need clean, aged water, so these should not be the first fish you buy. Add neons or cardinals when the tank has been running for a few weeks.

❖ *Neon tetras*

▎ **Emperor tetra** *(Nematobrycon palmeri)*

Emperor tetra facts
- ■ *Length:* 5 cm (2 in)
- ■ *Aquarium size:* 75 cm (2½ ft) ■ *pH:* 5–8
- ■ *Staple diet:* tropical flake
- ■ *Swims:* midwater ■ *Spawning:* egg layers

The emperor tetra is another example of the variety and beauty of the tetras. Although not as flashy as the neons and cardinals, this is nonetheless a fish that will enhance any tetra community. Often appearing dull in the bright exposed conditions of

❖ *Emperor tetra*

aquarium shops, the fish will come into its own in a well-planted tank with dark gravel and low light, when it reveals itself to be a deep purple. This peaceful tetra will flourish in a quiet community – it is a fish that would be even more popular if specimens in shops were not nearly always seen at a disadvantage.

CHAPTER
THREE

Congo tetra *(Phenacogrammus interruptus)*

Congo tetra facts
- *Length:* 9 cm (3½ in)
- *Aquarium size:* 1 m (3 ft) ■ *pH:* 6–7
- *Staple diet:* tropical flake
- *Swims:* midwater ■ *Spawning:* egg layers

Although the congo tetra is larger than those previously described, it is equally peaceful and will fit into a larger quiet community well. It prefers a dark environment in which its iridescent colours will show up best. Congo tetras are naturally shy but will acquire confidence from an absence of bright lighting and being kept in a reasonably-sized shoal of at least six individuals.

❖ *Congo tetras*

Zebra danio and Leopard danio
(Brachydanio rerio)

Zebra and leopard danio facts
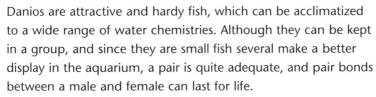

- **Length:** 6 cm (2½ in)
- **Aquarium size:** 1 m (3 ft) ■ **pH:** 6–8
- **Staple diet:** tropical flake
- **Swims:** midwater ■ **Spawning:** egg layers

Danios are attractive and hardy fish, which can be acclimatized to a wide range of water chemistries. Although they can be kept in a group, and since they are small fish several make a better display in the aquarium, a pair is quite adequate, and pair bonds between a male and female can last for life.

The zebra danio, as its name suggests, is handsomely liveried in black and white stripes, whereas the leopard is spotted in

❖ *Zebra danios*

brown. Although the two look very different, they are actually both the same species. Even though the leopard danio was assigned a scientific name, *Brachydanio frankei*, it is just a colour variation of the zebra. For this reason it is unwise to keep the two together if you would like to spawn them.

Rainbowfish

Australian blue-eye *(Pseudomugil signifer)*
- *Length:* 4 cm (1¾ in)
- *Aquarium size:* 60 cm (2 ft) ■ *pH:* 7
- *Staple diet:* live or frozen food, flakes
- *Swims:* midwater ■ *Spawning:* egg layers

Celebes rainbowfish *(Marosatherina ladigesi)*
- *Length:* 7.5 cm (3 in)
- *Aquarium size:* 75 cm (2½ ft) ■ *pH:* 7–8
- *Staple diet:* live or frozen food, flakes
- *Swims:* midwater ■ *Spawning:* egg layers

Lake Kutubu rainbowfish *(Melanotaenia lacustris)*
- *Length:* 10 cm (4 in)
- *Aquarium size:* 1 m (3 ft) ■ *pH:* 7–8
- *Staple diet:* live or frozen food, flakes
- *Swims:* midwater ■ *Spawning:* egg layers

Rainbowfish come in a wide variety of colours, but all of them are exceptionally beautiful and, ranging in size from the tiny Australian blue-eye to larger fishes of around 15cm (6 in), a suitable fish can be found for most sizes of aquarium.

❖ *Rainbowfish*

All are peaceful fish that prefer to shoal with others of their kind, and a group of six or so will provide a brilliant display. Rainbowfish prefer live foods, but most will accept a diet of flakes provided it is well supplemented with live or frozen live foods. The appearance of the fish will more than compensate for any inconvenience in providing a healthy diet. Regardless of your taste in colours, one of the rainbowfish is bound to impress you. The delicate yellow and black markings of the Celebes rainbowfish, the iridescent blues of the blue rainbowfish and the flashing yellow fins and brilliant blue eyes of the Australian blue-eye are just a few of the most spectacular naturally coloured fish available to hobbyists. Many will breed easily in the aquarium, leaving their eggs in fine-leaved plants, such as java fern, or wool mops provided for the purpose by the aquarist. Rainbowfish prefer hard water.

Harlequin rasbora *(Rasbora heteromorpha)*

Harlequin rasbora facts
- **Length:** 4 cm (1¾ in)
- **Aquarium size:** 60 cm (2 ft) ■ **pH:** 5–7
- **Staple diet:** tropical flake
- **Swims:** midwater ■ **Spawning:** egg layers

The Harlequin is attractive, active and peaceful, and a good choice for a community aquarium with small fish. These fish will feel insecure in bright lights or alone; they need a dark, planted tank and to have at least seven or so fellows to shoal with. In these

❖ *Harlequin rasbora*

conditions they will show their colours best; a fish that looks bland and uninteresting in bright lights will appear at its best when feeling secure. In the wild these fishes feed on crustaceans, worms and insects, so will appreciate live foods (as do most fish!)

CHAPTER
THREE

▌ Dwarf gourami *(Colisa lalia)*

Dwarf gourami facts
- *Length:* 5 cm (2 in)
- *Aquarium size:* 60 cm (2 ft) ▪ *pH:* 6–8
- *Staple diet:* tropical flake
- *Swims:* midwater ▪ *Spawning:* eggs, parental care

The male dwarf gourami is strikingly attractive, being banded in iridescent red and blue stripes. Some varieties can be found in which the red or blue dominates, with only traces or none at all of the other colour. The females are, unfortunately, small and grey.

In the aquarium you should either keep a single male, or a male with two females (as he can be a bully towards his wives if one is not ready to mate, and with two the aggression is dissipated). Gouramis build bubble nests in which to lay their eggs, and will become frustrated and unhappy in a tank with a strong current where the bubble nest is continually being destroyed by the current.

❖ *Male dwarf gourami*

Opaline or Three-spot gourami
(Trichogaster trichopterus)

Opaline or Three-spot gourami facts
- **Length:** 10 cm (4 in)
- **Aquarium size:** 60 cm (2 ft) ■ **pH:** 6–8
- **Staple diet:** tropical flake
- **Swims:** midwater ■ **Spawning:** egg layers

Also known as the blue gourami, this fish is peaceful despite being fairly large. Although only one male should be kept, the fish will cohabit peacefully with other quiet fishes. The common name of 'three-spot' gourami can confuse people when they first see the fish, as there are only two! The third 'spot' of the name refers to the eye. Hardy and tolerant, the three-spot gourami is attractively patterned in a bright blue with darker markings. However, don't rely on this fish to add movement to your tank –

❖ *Opaline*

they are notorious for being very sedentary. This means, however, that they are suitable for a slightly smaller aquarium than normal for a fish of this size. Like all gouramis, they are capable of breathing air and build bubble nests in which to lay their eggs, so they will need a tank with only a little water movement.

As with many fish that have been kept in aquaria for a long time, there are several variations of the normal colouring available, including some that no longer have the spots and some that are an attractive yellow instead of blue.

CHAPTER
THREE

Gold barb or Schubert's barb
(Puntius semifasciolatus)

Gold barb facts
- *Length:* 10 cm (4 in)
- *Aquarium size:* 1 m (3 ft) ■ *pH:* 6–8
- *Staple diet:* tropical flake
- *Swims:* midwater ■ *Spawning:* egg layers

The gold barb is a good fish for a larger aquarium. It is a peaceful shoaling fish that needs to be kept in a group to look its best. They are robust and easy to keep with metallic scales which will gleam to good effect in the aquarium.

❖ *Gold barb*

Tiger barb *(Puntius tetrazona)*

Tiger barb facts
- *Length:* 7.5 cm (3 in)
- *Aquarium size:* 75 cm (2½ ft) ■ *pH:* 6–8
- *Staple diet:* tropical flake
- *Swims:* midwater ■ *Spawning:* egg layers

The tiger barb has been a popular aquarium inhabitant for a long time, but a little caution needs to be exercised before adding these to the community tank. These are quite aggressive fish, so you may think it better to only keep a few. This is completely the wrong approach, as a solitary tiger barb will have nothing better to do than pick on other aquarium inhabitants. In a large group, they spend their time quarrelling amongst themselves and ignore other fishes. Nonetheless, this would be an unwise tankmate for very quiet fishes, or those with trailing fins, such as guppies. A shoal of these fish is ideal for anyone who likes a lot of movement in their tank – the tigers will always be out and about. The natural colour of the fish is orange with four black stripes vertically down the body. There are also other colour varieties including the green tiger barb and pale orangey pink albino fish.

❖ *Tiger barb*

Odessa barb *(cf. Puntius ticto)*

Odessa barb facts
- ■ **Length:** 10 cm (4 in)
- ■ **Aquarium size:** 1 m (3 ft) ■ **pH:** 6–8
- ■ **Staple diet:** tropical flake
- ■ **Swims:** midwater ■ **Spawning:** egg layers

The Odessa barb is extremely striking: most of the body is silvery, but each scale is outlined in deep black. The males have a brilliant swathe of red along the side. This peaceful shoaling fish is very active and probably not suited for a tank of shy fish. With lots of swimming space a shoal will make a spectacular display. The Odessa is likely to be a variant of the two-spot barb, *Puntius ticto*, which is very similar but not as bright in its colouring. The Odessa barb emerged directly into the aquarium market and is reputed to have originated in Odessa.

❖ *Odessa barb*

CHAPTER
THREE

CICHLIDS

All cichlids are territorial and prone to aggression when spawning and guarding fry, but the species recommended here are peaceful the rest of the time and are small enough to be accommodated in a community tank without bloody warfare erupting at spawning time. They are best kept in pairs – the best way to get a pair is to buy several youngsters and grow them on until a pair develops, when the spares can be returned to the shop or exchanged with other aquarists.

Krib *(Pelvicachromis pulcher)*

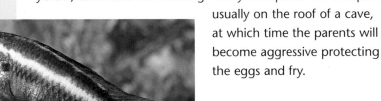

Krib facts
- *Length:* 10 cm (4 in)
- *Aquarium size:* 60 cm (2 ft) if sole inhabitants, else 1 m (3 ft) ■ *pH:* 6.5–7.5
- *Staple diet:* tropical flake
- *Swims:* midwater ■ *Spawning:* eggs, parental care

The krib's small size and relatively peaceful temperament makes a pair a practical proposition in the community. Their latin name means 'beautiful' and they are, being a purplish colour with yellow, black and red markings. They will spawn in the aquarium, usually on the roof of a cave, at which time the parents will become aggressive protecting the eggs and fry.

Left: *Although all beautiful, kribs originating from different regions show some variations in colour and pattern.*

Bolivian ram *(Microgeophagus altispinosus)*

Bolivian ram facts
- **Length:** 7.5 cm (3 in)
- **Aquarium size:** 60 cm (2 ft) if sole inhabitants, else 1 m (3 ft) ■ **pH:** 6–7.5
- **Staple diet:** tropical flake
- **Swims:** midwater ■ **Spawning:** eggs, parental care

The Bolivian ram is an attractive, although not so brightly coloured, cousin of the ordinary ram, *Microgeophagus ramirezi*. However, whereas ordinary rams can be delicate and insist on soft water, the Bolivian ram is a more resilient fish that will adjust to harder waters with greater ease.

❖ *Bolivian ram*

African butterfly cichlid
(Anomalochromis thomasi)

African butterfly cichlid facts
- ■ *Length:* 10 cm (4 in)
- ■ *Aquarium size:* 60 cm (2 ft) if sole inhabitants, else 1 m (3 ft) ■ *pH:* 6.5–7
- ■ *Staple diet:* tropical flake
- ■ *Swims:* midwater ■ *Spawning:* eggs, parental care

Like the rams and kribs, this is a relatively peaceful fish which only becomes aggressive when spawning. The spawn is attached to a flat stone or other surface in the open, so the parents are particularly diligent about guarding the exposed eggs.

Above: *This spawning pair of attractive African butterfly cichlids are from Zaire.*

Sheepshead acara *(Aequidens curviceps)*

Sheepshead acara facts
- **Length:** 7.5 cm (3 in)
- **Aquarium size:** 60 cm (2 ft) if sole inhabitants, else 1 m (3 ft) ■ **pH:** 6.5–7.5
- **Staple diet:** tropical flake
- **Swims:** midwater ■ **Spawning:** eggs, parental care

The sheepshead acara is a small and peaceful member of a family that also includes some of the biggest bullies of the aquarium world, such as the aptly named 'green terror' *(Aequidens rivulatus)*. It is therefore quite important that the specialist shop where you buy them knows exactly what it is you want! The sheepshead is a beautiful iridescent greenish blue with black markings, including an upward curving line across the mouth that looks endearingly like a permanent smile. They spawn on flat, open surfaces and, true to their cichlid nature, will become aggressive at this time, but the normally shy fish will appreciate lots of plants to make them feel secure.

Right: *These sheepshead acaras are raising a family and carefully guarding their eggs.*

CHAPTER
THREE

▌LOACHES

A wide variety of loaches make their appearance in aquarium shops, some of which are more suitable than others so caution needs to be exercised. The Siamese algae eater, or sucking loach, is a particularly unpleasant creature often sold for algae control. Unfortunately, it grows large and territorial, and can develop an unwholesome preference for meat rasped off the sides of its living tankmates. Others, notably those of the botia family, are renowned for fin nipping and making life a general misery for their companions. The two recommended here, however, are peaceful and attractive.

❖ *Kuhlii loach*

▌Kuhlii loach *(Pangio kuhlii)*

Kuhlii loach facts
- *Length:* 10 cm (4 in)
- *Aquarium size:* 60 cm (2 ft)   ■ *pH:* 6–7.5
- *Staple diet:* sinking pellets
- *Swims:* bottom   ■ *Spawning:* egg layers

The kuhlii loach adds interest to a tank, although not always high visibility. It is a master of concealment, and sometimes will not be seen for months on end, burrowing in the gravel or lurking in plants. Nonetheless, it does not take up much space and will excite comment when it does appear, being decidedly un-fishlike. The long elongated body appears more like a snake than a fish, and bands of bright orange and black make it even more noteworthy. Kuhliis in shops may actually be from one of several species (some are not even black and orange), but all can be kept in similar conditions and with similar ease.

Clown loach *(Botia macracanthus)*

Clown loach facts
- *Length:* 17.5 cm (7 in);
  30 cm (12 in) in the wild
- *Aquarium size:* 1.2 m (4 ft) ■ *pH:* 6–7.5
- *Staple diet:* sinking pellets
- *Swims:* bottom and midwater ■ *Spawning:* egg layers

The clown loach is another striking black and orange fish, but much more visible than the kuhlii. These shoaling fish need to be kept in groups, and they will be constantly out and about in the tank, often indulging in endearing acrobatics. A less endearing habit is that of playing dead; a fish lying on its side is not necessarily sick – sometimes they just like adopting that position. They are also reputed to devour snails in the aquarium, thus making themselves useful as well as attractive. The need to keep a group of relatively large fish makes them impractical for smaller aquaria.

❖ *Clown loach*

▌CATFISH

The catfishes comprise one of the largest and most varied families of fishes, with over 2000 species. They live in both inland and coastal waters of nearly every continent, excluding only the inhospitable far North and South. Some giants grow to several metres, but from such a large family it is unsurprising that there are lots of smaller species which are ideal for the aquarium.

▌Dwarf otocinclus *(Otocinclus affinis)*

Dwarf otocinclus facts
- ▪ **Length:** 4 cm (1½ in)
- ▪ **Aquarium size:** 60 cm (2 ft) ▪ **pH:** 5–7.5
- ▪ **Staple diet:** algae pellets, lettuce, cucumber and other vegetables
- ▪ **Swims:** bottom ▪ **Spawning:** egg layers

Many aquariums are afflicted by algae in the early days, and even well-kept established ones often acquire a coating of 'green fuzz'. Otocinclus are the smallest effective algae eater available, and ideal for a small tank. Otocinclus are members of the Loricariidae, a family of catfish which have mouths specially adapted to form suckers, often armed with grinding teeth. The fish are flattened in shape, and the mouth is located on the bottom of the body. In many species this configuration has proved ideal to make

❖ *Dwarf otocinclus*

them efficient algae removers. These are peaceful, tiny fish and, as such, they need similarly small and peaceful tank mates, and dense plant cover to make them feel safe. For larger aquaria and those with more active fish, the bristlenose catfish (see right) would be a better choice. Otocinclus will be happiest if there is a small group of them, although they will not necessarily remain in one another's company all the time.

▌ Bristlenose catfish *(Ancistrus species)*

Bristlenose facts
- ▪ *Length:* 10 cm (4 in)
- ▪ *Aquarium size:* 1 m (3 ft) ▪ *pH:* 6–8
- ▪ *Staple diet:* algae pellets, lettuce, cucumber and other vegetables
- ▪ *Swims:* bottom ▪ *Spawning:* eggs, parental care

The bristlenose catfish is another member of the Loricariidae, and an equally efficient algae remover. At 10 cm (4 in), though, they are rather more sturdy than Otocinclus, and suitable for a more busy aquarium. Like most of the loricariids, the skin of the exposed back and sides is formed of hard, bony plates called scutes (which means 'shield' in Latin). This covering will keep them safe from the attentions of fish such as the cichlids (see

▌ **Above:** *This male bristlenose shows the flourishing growth of soft bristles that give these fish their common name.*

CHAPTER
THREE

▌ **Above:** *This young bristlenose is either a female or too young to have grown the bushy 'bristles'.*

page 66), which may perceive a fish grazing over the substrate as a threat to eggs (not without reason).

Although bristlenoses will happily take an egg breakfast they will not harm any living fishes. Dead ones are another matter, and their caretaking duties will include the speedy removal of any corpses, which eventually occur in even the best kept aquarium.

The male bristlenose is remarkable for the mass of soft fleshy bristles on the nose, which appear rather as though a small soft bush had grown there. Male bristlenoses are mildly territorial towards one another, and best kept as a pair.

❖ *Whiptail catfish*

Whiptail catfish

Rineloricaria parva facts
- *Length:* 11 cm (4½ in)
- *Aquarium size:* 1 m (3 ft) ■ *pH:* 6–7.8
- *Staple diet:* Vegetables, algae wafers
- *Swims:* bottom ■ *Spawning:* eggs, parental care

Sturisoma aureum facts
- *Length:* 55 cm (22 in)
- *Aquarium size:* 1 m (3 ft) ■ *pH:* 6–8
- *Staple diet:* Vegetables, algae wafers
- *Swims:* bottom ■ *Spawning:* eggs, parental care

├─20 CM (8 IN)─┤

Many species of loricariid catfish are commonly referred to as whiptails; all share the characteristic of a long tail which makes them bear a striking resemblance to twigs. Most species are not brightly coloured, although some of them can be striking; there is a red whiptail, and many have black patterning. Whatever is lacking in colour is made up for by interest in the aquarium; like many of the loricariids they appear decidedly unfishlike lying along bogwood trying to blend in or working their way over the substrate or glass. Most catfish sold as whiptails are either *Loricaria*, *Rineloricaria* or *Sturisoma* species.

Although many species look very similar, even to experts, all are good inhabitants for a community aquarium and can be kept either singly or as a pair. Many have been bred in the aquarium. If you would like to try, look out for a male with a crop of spiky bristles growing at the sides of the mouth. These only appear on males in breeding condition, so if you see one of these you know that it is a healthy male. Whiptails eat vegetable foods, and although they do eat algae they require other vegetables, such as lettuce, courgette and spinach, to stay fit and well.

CHAPTER
THREE

▌ Glass catfish *(Kryptopterus bicirrhis)*

Glass catfish facts
- ■ *Length:* 15 cm (6 in)
- ■ *Aquarium size:* 1 m (3 ft) ■ *pH:* 6–7.5
- ■ *Staple diet:* tropical flake
- ■ *Swims:* midwater ■ *Spawning:* egg layers

It is easy to see how the glass catfish came by its name – these fish are completely transparent except for the spine and the body organs which occupy a small space just behind the head. These shoaling fish are ethereally beautiful, although not brightly coloured. Although they are peaceful, 15 cm (6 in) is quite a large fish and they will track down and eat fry or anything small enough to fit into their mouths. They prefer a strong current in the aquarium, such as that provided by a power filter directed along the tank.

❖ *Glass catfish*

❖ *Upside-down catfish*

Upside-down catfish *(Synodontis nigriventris)*

Upside-down catfish facts
- **Length:** 10 cm (4 in)
- **Aquarium size:** 1 m (3 ft) ■ **pH:** 7–8
- **Staple diet:** tropical flake, pellets
- **Swims:** midwater ■ **Spawning:** eggs, parental care

The upside-down catfish is remarkable for the way in which it swims. While most fish have dark backs and pale stomachs, the upside-down catfish has a pale back and a dark stomach, and habitually swims the wrong way up. This is only one member of a large family, of which several others also swim in this strange way. *Synodontis nigriventris* is one of the smaller species, and also a peaceful aquarium inhabitant. The fish will appreciate a planted tank, in which they will browse the undersides of leaves and décor looking for microscopic creatures to eat. They are not shoaling fish, but peaceful with their own kind, so the aquarist can choose to keep an individual, a pair or a group.

CHAPTER
THREE

▋Corydoras

Corydoras facts
■ *Length:* Bronze, 7.5 cm (3 in)
Pepper cory, 5 cm (2 in)
■ *Aquarium size:* 1 m (3 ft) ■ *pH:* 5.8–7.5
■ *Staple diet:* sinking pellets
■ *Swims:* bottom ■ *Spawning:* egg depositors

Corydoras are one of the most endearing catfish, and as they remain small are ideal for most community aquaria. Many people will be tempted to buy some of these after believing one winked at them in the shop; this is due to their ability to move their eyes independently, but definitely adds to their charm. Corydoras are shoaling fish, and are best seen in a group of at least six; this way they are more likely to be seen out and about in the aquarium.

The Corydoras comprise a large number of South American species, including some which are particular about their water chemistry. However, two of the most popular species, the Bronze (*Corydoras aeneus*) and the Pepper cory (*Corydoras paleatus*) are not only cute but very adaptable. These have been bred in

L-number and C-numbered fish

Sometimes in an aquarium shop you may see a loricariid (suckermouth), or Corydoras, with a number instead of a name. This system was originated by DATZ, a German magazine, to provide a system of identification for all the new catfishes being discovered and appearing in shops without identifying names. In general, unless you specialize in catfish it's better to buy well-known species. The new numbered fish are likely to be very expensive, and you may have difficulty finding out how best to keep them.

❖ *Pepper cory*

aquarists' tanks many times, and are nearly always available in the aquarium shop. Most of the specimens in the aquarium shops are bred in farms in Singapore. Occasionally you may see wild-caught fish, which are often even more beautiful. Albino pepper corys are also common, and can provide a striking contrast with other fish in the tank. All Corydoras are very peaceful and will cause no trouble either among their own group or with other aquarium inhabitants. Catfish pellets provide a good staple diet, but to keep them in peak condition they will appreciate some meaty foods, such as frozen live foods or shredded shrimp, as a supplement to their meals. Like many catfish, Corydoras are able to use atmospheric air, and will make repeated trips to the surface in polluted or stagnant water to breathe air. However, this is only a cause for worry if the trips to the surface are frequent, as they do this to a lesser extent as a matter or course; often one fish heading up for air will inspire the others in the shoal to do likewise.

CHAPTER FOUR

The planted aquarium

Although some fish come from rivers and lakes where plants are in very short supply, most people prefer an aquarium that features at least a few plants. Although some are hard to grow and have special requirements, many plants will grow easily and add interest and beauty to the aquarium scene.

Real or plastic plants?

Most aquaria will look better for including some plants. Plastic plants are undoubtedly easier to keep, and are available in a variety of colours ranging from very natural and lifelike choices to luminous neon colours. Apart from being impossible to kill, another advantage of plastic plants is that your careful arrangements will always remain the same. Leaves will not fall, they will not grow and require pruning, and new little plantlets will not suddenly appear in places you had not intended them to be. However, to many aquarists this growth and change is one of the most attractive features about their tank; that the aquarium is a natural living and changing environment. Real plants add an extra dimension as they grow, die back, multiply and even occasionally flower!

■ **Opposite:** *Hi fin red tuxedo swordtail*

CHAPTER
FOUR

Above: *Plastic plants are now very lifelike and can make a beautiful aquarium display.*

The role of plants in the natural cycle

Natural plants not only look attractive in the tank but perform a useful function as well. Plants, like all other living things, need to eat, and they do this by extracting food from the water and substrate. This food is the end product of the biological filtration and wastes of the fishes. If you have lots of fish and no plants, the water will become full of nutrients unless you change it frequently. Nature, as they say, abhors a vacuum, and the empty role in your aquarium will be rapidly filled by the easiest-to-grow plant of all – algae. Although the fish don't object to algae, few people find an aquarium attractive with green water and the glass and décor covered in green slime. A well-planted tank will be much less prone to outbreaks of the dreaded algae plague.

Choosing plants

In any aquarium shop there will be lots of plants in a wide variety of shades of green and even red, of differing heights, and a correspondingly wide range of prices. What is not immediately apparent to the beginner is that many of these plants are not really suitable for the normal community tank.

■ Many require high light levels (especially the red ones) and need a lot more than the single fluorescent tube fitted to the average tank.

■ Others, which are often the first to be bought as they look very attractive, are actually not water plants at all. Little palm trees, Dracaena (dragon tree), and many others fall into this category. These are guaranteed to bring eventual disappointment as they die (although it is a cheap way of getting a nice house plant if you buy a pot and plant it properly).

■ Feathery plants, such as myriophyllum, have a tendency to be ripped to pieces by all but the most placid fish.

■ Many rooted plants will object strongly to the water movement around their roots caused by an undergravel filter.

Fortunately, the problem of the undergravel can be overcome easily, and there are enough suitable plants to make an attractive natural aquarium well within the reach of even the most 'brown-fingered' aquarist.

Plants as oxygenators

Plants are often added as 'oxygenators' to increase the level of oxygen in the water. However, while they do breathe in carbon dioxide and breathe out oxygen during the day, at night the plants reverse the process and will actually consume oxygen from the water. There must be enough oxygen in your tank for both the plants and the fish!

CHAPTER
FOUR

▌Suitable plants for beginners

Java fern

Java fern, *Microsorium pteropus*, is an amazingly tough and hardy plant. The dark green elongated leaves are tough and bitter to the taste, so the plant will be ignored by the most rapacious of vegetarian fish. It is suitable for both temperate and tropical aquaria, and will thrive in the light provided by a single fluorescent tube. Not only is the plant easy to grow, but it can also be grown attached to bogwood or other décor with a suitably rough surface for the roots to find an attachment. New plants can be held in place by rubber bands or wedged into position until the growing roots find a hold. Avoid using black cotton, as is sometimes recommended, as some spiky fish, such as bristlenoses, can become entangled and die.

Once Java fern has established itself, it will rapidly reproduce. The original plant will spread out, and new plants can be broken away deliberately from the main mass or will detach themselves spontaneously. The plants also produce new tiny plantlets from the edges of older leaves – often those that look as though they

❖ *Java fern*

are dying back, so excessive neatening and pruning will have the undesirable result of preventing the new plantlets forming.

Anubias species

Anubias plants come in a variety of species, which range from tall background plants to the low-growing *Anubias nana*. All have dark green, shiny leaves which look attractive in the aquarium, but leaf shapes vary between species, from

❖ *Anubias nana*

the elongated leaves of *Anubias lanceolata* to the oval leaves of *Anubias barteri*.

Like Java fern, Anubias are not in the least perturbed by water movement around their roots, and they will thrive happily in undergravel filters or attached to bogwood or other pieces of décor. You can sometimes buy them preattached, complete with bogwood, but this tends to be an expensive option and it is cheaper to just buy the plants and hold them in place until they attach themselves.

Although Anubias are relatively slow growing, they are hardy and easy to keep and will often reward the aquarist with a flower spike. These flowers are not very decorative, being greenish white and of a similar shape to those of the Arum lily (but not, unfortunately, of such an impressive size). Although they flower in the aquarium, plants from seed are hard to achieve, and it is easier to obtain new plants by dividing the old ones when they grow big enough. Long horizontal roots can be

CHAPTER
FOUR

cut with a razor blade or sharp knife to divide the plant. Anubias are happy in relatively low light but are only suitable for the tropical aquarium.

Cryptocorynes

Cryptocorynes also thrive happily in less light than most fish but do need to be planted properly. If you are using an undergravel filter, it is better to plant them in small pots with a suitable growing medium. The top of the soil should be covered with gravels to stop it escaping into the aquarium. Planting in this way has the additional advantage of allowing you to rearrange your plants if required by just moving the pots, instead of having to disturb the roots. Crypts are particularly unhappy about being moved, and new plants often die back quickly when placed in the aquarium. However, if the dead leaves are removed (to prevent them rotting in the tank and placing an additional load on the filtration), new growth will soon start to appear.

Many plants for the aquarium trade are really bog plants, and are grown by the dealers out of water. When placed in the water they will soon adjust, but this usually involves all the old leaves dying and new underwater leaves growing. Don't assume that your new plants are past all help too quickly; often most of the existing leaves will be lost before the plant settles in and starts growing anew. Cryptocorynes are suitable only for the tropical tank and grow better in soft water conditions.

Java moss

The dark green fronds of Java moss are attractive, easy to grow and versatile in the aquarium. The moss does not need to be rooted and can be left free-floating in the tank. However, if you want it to stay in one place, fasten it where you want it with a rubber band or weight it down with some lead plant weight. The moss will quickly attach itself and thereafter remain where it was

Right: *Java moss is ideal for sheltering fry from rapacious parents. This clump is being used for this purpose in a swordtail tank.*

put. It is useful as well as attractive: if you want to try breeding your fish (or the fish decide to do so themselves) then the fry will be able to shelter in the moss and avoid the depredations of the parents and other fish in the tank.

Planting the tank

Try to plan how you want your tank to look before you actually start buying plants. Consider the eventual height your plants will reach; although sometimes a single large plant in the foreground can be effective, usually the tallest plants are best kept at the back and sides, with smaller low-growing ones at the front. In nature, most plants grow in groups, rather than as single specimens of each species, so your tank will look more natural if you have groups of plants of a few types, rather than lots of different ones.

Treat your new plants with the same consideration as you give your new fish: don't let them get chilled or squashed on the way back from the shop, and put them into their final positions as quickly as possible. Many plants are sold in plastic pots, which look unsightly and can restrict root growth, but if you remove the pots be careful not to damage the roots. Damaged plants will be much slower to settle in than those that are treated carefully.

CHAPTER FIVE

Running your aquarium

Now that you have set up your equipment and chosen the fish you would like to own, it only remains for you to add them to their new home. With only a little care and effort, your aquarium will soon be a focal point of your home, providing a continually changing picture.

▌Your new fish

Once your tank is set up and all the equipment installed, you will want to see it full of fish as quickly as possible. However, the temptation to return from the shop with full bags of fish must be resisted. Biological filtration depends on a healthy growth of bacteria to work, but, of course, while there are no fish there is no waste and no food for the bacteria, so there will not be many of them. If you buy all your fish at once, then they will start producing waste straight away, and the sparse bacteria will not be able to clear it all up. By buying the first fishes one at a time, you ensure that the waste in the aquarium does not suddenly shoot up to toxic levels overnight. One fish only produces a bit of waste, and the bacteria will multiply with the new food source and soon reach a level where

■ **Opposite:** *A red male Siamese fighting fish.*

the single fish's wastes are being filtered effectively. You can then add another fish, and once again the bacteria increase to cope. Repeat the procedure until your tank is fully stocked.

This does not work so well if the fish you have chosen are large (as the waste produced by one large fish will be equivalent to that produced by lots of little ones) or if you want shoaling fish. If you

Buying fish

When you buy your fish, have a look round the shop first, and check whether the fish in the tanks seem healthy and active. If there seem to be lots of fish that are pale, inactive, obviously diseased or even dead, then do not buy your fish there, even if the one you want seems to be healthy. You should take care especially not to buy fish from a tank in which some of the others seem unwell. Although some of the fish may not seem to show the same symptoms, they might get sick after you buy them, and might even infect all the fish you already have.

Of course, different fish behave in different ways normally, and you should read about the fish you want to buy before going to the shop, so that you know what colour they are supposed to be and how they should behave. For example, if you have chosen a species that is supposed to be nocturnal, it would be unreasonable to expect them to be swimming about when you visit the shop.

When buying fish, try to visit during the week; often shops have part-time staff at the weekend who may not be as knowledgeable about the fish, and may be inexperienced at catching them. Your new fish is bound to suffer some stress as it moves to your tank, but this can be made much worse by inexperienced people chasing them round and round a tank to catch them. Once you have chosen and bought your fish, take it home as quickly as possible; the aquarium shop should always be the last stop on your shopping trip.

want species that prefer to be kept together, the first fish to be added will be alone while the filter gets started, and will be frightened and unhappy. It is better to buy two or three, and give the filter a helping hand to get going by adding some filter starter in accordance with the instructions.

While you are stocking the tank and the filters are adjusting, it is very important to test the tank regularly (daily) for ammonia and nitrites (see page 96). Only when the ammonia and nitrite concentrations have remained at zero for a couple of days should you consider adding the next fish, and if the ammonia or nitrite concentration reaches danger level you will need to change some of the water with dechlorinated tap water.

Introducing fish into the aquarium

When you arrive home with your fish, it will be nervous and upset. Fish dislike sudden change, and if the water in your tank is a different temperature to the water to which it is accustomed, this will upset the fish even more. Float the bag inside the tank for an hour, so that the water in the bag can slowly reach the same temperature as that in the tank. Leave the lights off at this time, as the fish will be much calmer in the dark. Once the temperature is the same, open the bag and hold it under the water so that the fish can swim out of its own accord. Leave the tank lights off and avoid feeding until the next day so that the fish has time to settle into its new home.

Feeding the fish

Feeding the fish should be an enjoyable time for both the aquarist and the fish. If you establish a regular routine the fish will come to know when it is feeding time and will be waiting in the place where you usually put the food in. Many fishes will quickly become used to the aquarist and will soon learn to take food from your hand.

The feeding time is also an ideal time for you to check that everything is well in the aquarium; often the first sign of any problems occurs when some or all of the fish are less than enthusiastic about their dinner than usual. Most of the fish will be in plain view at this time, and you will be able to inspect them to make sure that there is no sign of disease or bullying. If any fish are missing that usually come to feed, check to make sure they are not dead. Even in the best aquaria fish die occasionally (fish get old, too) and if the corpses are left they will decay and pollute the water.

In most community aquariums there is a variety of fish with different feeding habits. Some fish will only feed at the surface; some will wait in midwater to catch the food as it falls past; and some will be bottom feeders which will only take food from the bottom of the tank. Often the bottom feeders will miss out if you only feed floating foods. Although many catfish are bought

Above: *Most loricariids feed from the bottom, and you will need to give them sinking food if they are not to go hungry.*

Right: *Otocinclus are good algae eaters but need feeding as well! This Otocinclus flexilis is enjoying a piece of lettuce.*

to help keep the tank clean, they deserve a good meal as well, and you must ensure that all the fish get a chance to eat some of the food. There are a variety of types of food to help with this: feeding a mixture of floating flake and sinking pellets will keep the top feeders busy while the pellets fall to the waiting mouths below.

If you have any fish that are nocturnal (active at night), or shy, they could easily miss out on food altogether. For shy fish, add food in more than one place in the tank so that

Above: *Loricariid catfishes are bottom feeders, but always hungry! This one can't wait for the pellets to sink.*

they do not have to join a scrum to get a mouthful. For nocturnal fish, you will need to add some food when you switch off the lights so that the others do not eat it all before the night shift wakes up.

Types of food

Although most of the commercial fish foods are designed to provide a complete balanced diet, fish like a change, too.

■ **Live food** The equivalent of a box of chocolates for fish is live food. Bags of daphnia or bloodworm will make a valuable supplement to their diet, and you will enjoy watching them chase around the tank. Any live food that you add should be poured into a net and rinsed under the tap before you feed them to the fish; a quick sniff at a live food bag you have just opened will quickly make the reason for this obvious. All living things produce wastes, and the small organisms the fish enjoy eating are no exception. In the closed environment of a plastic bag this quickly reaches smelly proportions. Although daphnia and bloodworm are hardy, you do not want this polluted water going in the fish tank. It is also a good idea to find out which day your local shop has live food delivered. After a few days the water gets to be too much even for the hardy crustaceans and insect larvae, and if it has been in the shop for too long you may find that the live food is nearly all dead. Always buy the live food from a reputable shop; wild caught organisms fished out of the local pond can include parasites and other animals that are undesirable and dangerous to your fish.

Above: *Most fish enjoy live foods, and these angelfish eating tubifex from a special worm holder are no exception.*

Above: *These sociable corydoras catfish are quite happy to share a food tablet stuck on the glass.*

■ **Frozen food** If you do not have a good supplier, frozen foods are an acceptable alternative for most fish. A variety of types can be bought: mosquito larvae, bloodworm, daphnia, and tubifex among others. An advantage of frozen food is that it has been sterilized so no unpleasant parasites or diseases can be carried to your fish by accident.

Little and often

Remember not to overfeed: if any food is left in the tank after five minutes of the fish feeding, then you have fed too much. Miss out the next feed and then feed less the next time until you are giving the correct amount.

As fish naturally feed constantly, getting tiny meals regularly throughout the day, they would prefer to have lots of small meals in the aquarium. This is impractical for most aquarists who have to go out to work, but two regular daily feeds should be manageable for most people.

CHAPTER
FIVE

▍The regular maintenance schedule

Although your fish will not take a lot of time to look after, establishing patterns that are as regular as possible will keep them healthier and make your job easier. It is better to perform maintenance jobs little and often rather than subject to your fish to a total spring clean occasionally. If you devote a few minutes to the tank every evening, then problems are unlikely to reach crisis proportion. Try to perform the following tasks at least once a week to keep your aquarium healthy.

Water testing
Test your water periodically for ammonia and nitrite. Remember that in a successful aquarium there should be none. If there are even traces of these chemicals it means that the filters are not working correctly, that your tank is overstocked, or that something has overloaded the filters – overfeeding or perhaps a dead fish. Clean the filters, cut down on the food, and consider whether your fish might have grown too big, or perhaps you just have too many. You need to remedy the problem while the tell-tale ammonia and nitrite levels are still low – if they rise to any appreciable amount your fish will soon become ill and may die.

Water changes
Water changes are important for the health of your fish. Although nitrate, the end product of biological filtration, is not very toxic, it still needs to be kept in check by water changes. Also it is likely that some evaporation of water will occur. As only water evaporates, and not trace elements and minerals, every time some water evaporates the remaining water will have a

▍**Opposite:** *With only a little time and effort on a regular basis, a tank of healthy fish and plants is not hard to achieve.*

CHAPTER
FIVE

slightly higher chemical concentration. Water changes will stop the water getting more and more concentrated, whereas just topping up to make up for the evaporation will not. You should try to change twenty per cent of the tank water every week, remembering to dechlorinate new tap water.

Filter cleaning

The filters are essential to the aquarium, and it is vital that they are kept clean so that the water can continue to pass through them. If the filters become clogged with solids then less water will pass through and be filtered. Undergravels are easiest to clean at the same time as the water is changed. A gravel vacuum consists of a siphon hose with a wider part at the bottom. When the water is siphoned out, the wider part is used to stir around in the gravel. The heavy gravel falls back into the tank, but the

lighter detritus is sucked up with the water and removed from the tank. It is not necessary to vacuum all the gravel every week; do a different part of the tank each time so that the whole area is kept tidy. If there are rocks or bogwood, occasionally lift them up and clean the gravel underneath; surprising amounts of detritus can collect there.

Power filter sponges also need to be cleaned. Remember that the sponge is home to the colony of bacteria which are the heart of the

Left: *Cleaning the gravel regularly is vital in order to maintain a healthy undergravel filter.*

biological filter. Like fish, bacteria will be poisoned by chlorine, so if you wash the sponge under the tap you will kill the filter. Instead, clean the filter at the same time as the water change, and rinse the sponge out in the water you have just removed from the tank. It is not necessary for the sponge to be squeaky clean; just squeeze it out a few times in the bucket of old water. Check that the filter inlets in the case are not blocked up with waste. You may need to rinse the case as well. Occasionally the filter pump impellor acquires a slimy coat which impedes it turning correctly. A quick wash for the impellor will ensure that the filter remains working properly.

Plant pruning

Although you will obviously want your plants to be healthy and grow well, sometimes they can grow too well. Keep an eye on them to make sure that they are not taking over the tank and leaving the fish nowhere to swim, and prune them if they are getting out of control. If plants get too big, you may be able to divide them and swap the discarded half with an aquarist friend for some of his surplus plants or fish.

Even the healthiest plants will occasionally have dead leaves, and these should be removed as soon as possible to avoid them decomposing in the tank.

Although not one you will have chosen, algae is also a plant, and if you have algae in the tank you need to keep an eye on it to make sure it does not take over. The long stringy forms (blanketweed) can be pulled out by hand if you see any, and you can remove any soft green film on the aquarium glass with a toothbrush or special algae cleaner. Occasionally a very hard type may appear in spots on the aquarium glass; this will need to be removed with a razor blade. Be careful not to scratch the glass when removing algae.

CHAPTER SIX

Breeding aquarium fish

Many aquarists decide that they would like to spawn their fish, but often the fish will make the decision for themselves. Many fish species will spawn readily in the community aquarium, giving their owner the chance to observe their courtship and mating behaviour and the pleasure of watching the tiny fry grow to adulthood. The confirmed hobbyist will soon acquire a collection of aquaria where the fish can be spawned and reared in a controlled way, but this chapter is more for the beginner with limited facilities who would still like to enjoy the fun of breeding fish.

Once your new fish have reached a reasonable size, you can then swap them with other fishkeepers, possibly at your local fish club, or trade them with your aquarium shop for something you need. Unless you have a few swimming pools handy, you will not be able to keep all the fish you breed, although, of course, some will probably become permanent inhabitants of your aquaria.

Opposite: *These beautiful kribs are easy to spawn in the aquarium, and offer the added attraction of giving the aquarist a chance to see the parents caring for their new family.*

CHAPTER
SIX

▌Equipment

Although if left to their own devices a few fry may survive in the community aquarium, the fry will be less likely to become snacks and easier to look after and feed if they are not raised in the main tank. You could set up a small tank especially for breeding fish (which could also be used as a quarantine tank and for many other purposes). However, in an emergency, any reasonably sized non-metallic receptacle can be pressed into service as a temporary home, including buckets.

Heaters and filters

If you are rearing tropical fish, you will need a separate heater to keep the fry warm. If you have a permanent rearing tank then you can set this up with an undergravel filter in the normal way and keep it going ready for any new arrivals. Canister power filters cannot be used, as they will not only filter out normal debris from the water, but will also filter out all your baby fish!

A 'sponge-on-a-stick' filter, used with an air pump, is ideal for tiny fry. The air pump is connected to a hollow tube running into a sponge, which then pulls the water through the sponge performing biological filtration. The sponge will also grow colonies of other tiny animals, and the fry will often feed off these. Filter starter can be used to get the sponge working biologically very quickly.

Feeding the fry

It is also a good idea to have some fry food ready; although many fry will eat ground up flake food, special fry food has a higher nutritional value and will help the little fish to grow well and stay healthy. The fish suggested here will all thrive on a fry food obtainable from your local shop, or other easily available foods. Some species of fish have more particular requirements, such as requiring live foods or being too tiny even to accept

Above: *Although some fish, such as these neon tetras, can only be bred by advanced aquarists, there are plenty of fish that are suitable for breeding for the beginner.*

powder fry food, so if you intend to try to spawn something different, find out as much as you can before the eggs hatch! When you are feeding the fry, only give a little food at a time to avoid uneaten food polluting the water. Very small feeds several times a day are much better than one big feed.

The rearing tank
Many species of fish are very prolific, and you will probably not have the facilities to rear all of the fry. Choose a few fry or eggs to move to your rearing tank. If you put hundreds of fish into a small tank because you do not want them to be eaten, then the end result will be the same: the tank will become overstocked and the water will become poisoned.

▌ Abandoned to chance

Many species of fish regard their responsibilities as being at an end as soon as the eggs are laid. These fish usually improve the

CHAPTER
SIX

chances that some of their fry, or baby fish, will survive by producing large quantities of eggs on the basis that at least a few out of the hundreds (or thousands!) will escape the waiting mouths of predators.

Eggs make just as tasty a snack as fry and are unable to evade the aquarist's net, so it is most effective to move the eggs to a new tank as soon as they are seen. A fungicide added to the water will help prevent egg fungus – when the eggs develop a cottonwool-like growth and die.

Goldfish

Goldfish spawn easily in the aquarium, and scatter hundreds of eggs liberally. Although they will spawn in a bare tank, they are more likely to do so if you put in lots of soft plants, such as elodea, or even make fake plants out of long bunches of wool. You will know that your goldfish are ready to spawn when the male fish develop white spots on the gill plates at the side of the head and on the thickened fin rays at the leading edge of the pectoral fins. These spots are called tubercles.

The males will begin chasing the fatter and tubercle-less females. After a few days' preparatory chasing, one or more males will succeed in chasing a female into the plants, and their continual pushing and shoving will eventually make her release her eggs. When the eggs are laid, the male fish then release sperm, which fertilizes the eggs.

Rather than trying to scrape the eggs off the plants, just choose a section of plant that has enough tiny yellowish-clear eggs, and

Left: *Matching a fish's aquarium closely to its natural habitat has many advantages. Here a Corydoras adolfoi fry uses its camouflage to good effect on this large stone.*

Above: *Many of these juvenile goldfish have not yet got their adult colouration and are still grey and brown.*

move that to the rearing tank. After a few days (depending on temperature – fish hatch quicker in warmer temperatures, but don't boil them in an effort to speed them up), the eggs will hatch.

You may not see the fry at first – the little fish are not fully developed and appear like tiny splinters of glass, often hanging on to the sides of the tank. After a few more days they will become free-swimming, and you will see them darting about in the water. When they start swimming, you can start feeding them. Goldfish grow surprisingly quickly, but don't be disappointed that they are all brownish-grey. Their beautiful colours will develop much later. In an aquarium, the fish will often start to change colour while they are only 5 mm (½ in) long, but if they are growing up in a cold pond they may remain brown for over a year.

CHAPTER
SIX

Corydoras catfish

The entertaining Corydoras catfish will often breed in an aquarium. Some species are harder to breed than others, but bronze, pepper and panda corydoras are happy to spawn even in harder water. Often they will start to spawn just after a water change, especially if the new water is slightly colder. This makes them think that the floods have come, and they spawn so that the fry will have the advantage of all the extra space and food that flooding brings.

One or more smaller males will start chasing a larger, fatter female. In a shoal this often inspires other Corydoras, and there may be several pairs or trios chasing around the tank. Eventually one of the males is successful; the pair assume a position with the female pressing her head into the male's side, stimulating him with her barbels. This is why fish whose barbels have been damaged are unlikely to spawn properly. The female lays one or more eggs, which she holds in a pouch made by holding her pelvic fins together, and they are fertilized by the male's sperm.

Above: *These three Corydora adolfoi males are all pursuing the female although only one will fertilize her eggs.*

Some research seems to indicate that the female may actually swallow the male's sperm, and it passes rapidly through her digestive tract emerging near the eggs.

After fertilization the fish rest, motionless, for a few seconds, and then the female sets off in search of a suitable place to put them. Eggs may be deposited on the aquarium glass, on rocks or on plants. This sequence of events is repeated until the female runs out of eggs – for the bronze corydoras this may be after hundreds have been laid, but panda corydoras will only lay twenty or so (which are, therefore, a lot harder for you to find!).

The eggs can be detached from the aquarium glass with a razor blade and sucked out with a siphon, or plants or rocks with their accompanying eggs can be moved to the rearing tank. It is best to use a sponge filter and not an undergravel in the rearing tank – the little fry can fall between pieces of gravel and die, so a bare glass bottom is best.

▌Responsible parenthood

Other species of egglaying fish try to give their offspring the best start in life by guarding the eggs, preventing other fish from eating them. In some species this extends to guarding the fry until they are big enough to fend for themselves, whereas others lose interest once the eggs have hatched.

Bristlenose catfish
When a bristlenose female is ready to spawn, she approaches the male in the cave or cranny where he has established his territory. In the depths of the cave, the female lays a cluster of up to a hundred or more eggs, resembling a bright orange raspberry. After discharging this essential duty, she leaves the proud father to do all the hard work, and shows no further interest. Over the next four to five days, the male guards the eggs diligently,

protecting them from attack by keeping them underneath his armoured body, and fanning water over them so that the growing fry inside the eggs have plenty of oxygen. He does not eat or move around the aquarium – every minute is devoted to looking after the eggs.

Eventually these efforts are rewarded and the tiny fry emerge. At first it is difficult to confirm that this has happened, as the little slivers of fish are still attached to their giant orange yolk sacs. Examination, however, shows that each egg now has a frantically waving tail. The father continues to guard the fry but they are adept escapees. One by one, they escape their father's guard, usually gathering together somewhere else. Often the patient male will be left, still not eating, guarding one or two remnants of the brood carefully and not realising that most of them have left home.

A few will survive if the spawn is left in the community tank, but once the tasty-looking little animated yolk sacs start adventuring, the other fish will eat most of them. To have more

Above: *The male bristlenose takes painstaking care of the bright orange eggs.*

success, move the male and his eggs to a rearing tank by slipping the cave where he has made his home into a water-filled plastic bag, and then out again into the new tank. Once they have hatched, the male will not harm any of the babies, but for his own sake it is best to return him to the community tank where he can have a decent meal freed from the responsibilities of fatherhood.

The new babies will not need to be fed until all the yolk sacs have been absorbed, and then they will eat the same food as their parents: cucumber, blanched lettuce, spinach or algae wafers. There should be food available for them all the time – any uneaten food should be removed at the next feeding time and replaced with fresh. The fry grow quickly, and some will have to be given away very quickly if the tank is not to be overstocked. Extra aeration from a powerful airpump will be appreciated – unlike their parents, the babies are unable to survive by using atmospheric air.

Kribs

Kribs (a shortened form of their now obsolete name of Kribensis) are relatively peaceful fish and can be kept easily in a community tank. However, when they spawn, the gentle and timid fish turn into warriors which will protect their offspring against all comers.

The eggs are usually laid in a cave, and after fertilization both male and female remain with the eggs, cleaning and guarding them. Once the fry hatch and become free swimming, they remain with their parents in a group. This not only enables the

Above: *The tiny newly hatched bristlenose fry are still attached to their yolk sacs, giving them a handy source of food for the first few days.*

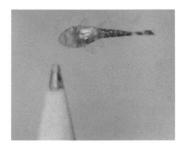

Above: *At a week old the yolk sac is gone and the fry, although still small, are feeding on the same foods as the adults and are self-sufficient.*

parents to protect them from other fish with relative ease – independent fry are short-lived ones – but it also helps you to feed them in the community tank. Mix up a solution of some water with some fry food and gently squirt it straight into the middle of the group with a turkey baster to ensure that it reaches the intended mouths.

Meanwhile, the other tank inhabitants will be coming to terms with life squashed up in the far end of the tank – they will not be allowed out until the krib family is starting to break up when the fry are old enough. You may wish to move the family, or to add a tank divider to give the other fish some peace. This parental behaviour is typical of all cichlids, not just kribs. Some are more aggressive, and many are bigger and require larger territories, making them unsuitable for the community. The only reason kribs can be kept as community fish is that they are too small to completely dominate a reasonably sized aquarium. If the other fish are not able to swim away the parent kribs will kill them, or die in the attempt. Cichlids are nonetheless fascinating, and many people will later move on from the community tank to specialize in this remarkable group of fish.

Livebearers

An alternative strategy to protecting the eggs outside the body is to protect them inside the body and give birth to live fish, which are born ready to swim away and escape predators. A large number of fish practise this method of egg defence, although some, like the sharks, are not suitable for the home aquarium! They are often referred to as a group ('livebearers') but this is in fact a misrepresentation. Many of the species are completely unrelated, and so it is not surprising that there are many biological differences between them. Some, such as guppies, are able to store sperm and use it to fertilize many batches of eggs, whereas others, such as platies, must mate every time fry are to be produced. Guppies merely retain the eggs inside their bodies, but do not nourish them as humans do with their placentas.

Nonetheless, some species do give added food to the fry as they grow. Goodeids, like the Crescent Zoe, have fry that attach themselves inside the mother by trophotaeniae, tiny filaments which perform the equivalent job of an umbilical cord. Like the umbilical in mammals, the trophotaeniae wither and fall away when the fry are born. Knowing this, it therefore makes sense that guppies give birth to lots of very small fry, whereas the goodeids produce a few large and well-fed ones.

Guppies, platies and swordtails

Guppies and platies are easy to keep and are almost guaranteed to breed in the aquarium. The females will nearly always be pregnant, and so it is easy to move one to a rearing tank on her own and wait – within a month you should have a tank full of fry. Whether the birth takes place in a rearing tank or within the community, there should always be lots of plants for the mother to hide in while she is giving birth, and where the fry can hide after they are born. If the female has to give birth in an exposed situation, she will be very stressed. For guppies the best sorts of plants are floating plant masses, as the fry dart for the surface as soon as they are born. Platies, however, head for the bottom

Right: *The stout platy is an attractive and easy-to-keep fish for everyone.*

and require lots of cover there. The tiny fry will start to feed almost immediately – and grow rapidly. After a couple of months they will be ready to give birth themselves.

You will know when a female is about to give birth as she will be immensely fat, almost square shaped and will try to get away from the other fish by hiding in plants or in corners. It is not a good idea to move a female at this stage to a separate tank as the stress of being caught and moved may damage her and even cause her to abort the fry. Some guppies show black areas near the tail, often referred to as a 'gravid spot', when they are pregnant. Others have a gravid spot all the time or not at all, so this is not the most reliable method of deciding whether a guppy is pregnant. In general, a livebearer will nearly always be pregnant if in good health and there is a male around, so if you want to move them do it while they are still slim. Plastic 'breeding traps' are sold for isolating pregnant livebearers. In practice, these terrify the life out of the fish, who cannot understand why they cannot get through the transparent plastic, and become dangerously stressed. It is better to let a fish give birth in the community tank and try to catch the fry later than to use one of these psychological torture boxes.

Careful breeding

The beautiful colour forms and fin shapes of these fish have been created by years of careful breeding. If you have a mixture of different types, then the offspring will vary widely and probably not be as nice as the parents. It is best to choose only one type of a species that you like, so that the fry have a known parentage. Furthermore, in the case of guppies, there is no point in choosing a particular type of male and female out of a shop tank filled with lots of different types. The female will almost certainly already be pregnant, and the fry could be fathered by any of the previous tankmates for several births to come. If you want to breed fish of a special variety, it is best to obtain them from a private dealer or fellow fishkeeper so that you can control their matings.

Conservation of fishes

Although the aquarium shop always seems to be stocked with an ever-increasing array of fish, many species are in danger. Most are threatened by the march of progress; swamp lands are being drained for farming and building, forests are cut down to provide revenue and farming space, and pollution decimates all but the toughest fish. Sometimes a new species of fish is introduced to an area where it is not native, and it proves better at surviving than the fishes that first lived there, using up the resources and pushing the natives into decline. Some fish are introduced deliberately – mosquitofish (Gambusia) have been introduced to many countries to control the breeding of malaria-carrying mosquitoes. Sometimes the introduction is merely an act of thoughtlessness as an irresponsible aquarist dumps fish he no longer wants into a pond or river.

There are many ways that you can help, some involving positive action and some merely involving a bit of thought.

■ Don't buy fish you won't be able to keep. If they are not really suited to your tank, leave them in the shop so that someone who will care for them

Right: *Cherry barbs, although common in aquarium shops, are now endangered in the natural habitat.*

will give them a home. This applies not just to giant rare catfish; no-one looking at tanks full of cherry barbs would imagine that these popular fish are endangered in their homeland.

■ If you make a mistake, try to find someone who would like your unwanted fish. Never just dump them in local ponds or rivers – there are fish that already live there and they don't want any new neighbours.

■ Where possible, try to keep a pair or a group and see if you can spawn them. Breeding fish is fun, and every little fish born in an aquarist's tank replaces one that need not be taken from the wild.

■ If you become interested in particular types of fish, such as livebearers, cichlids or catfish, consider joining a national club of fellow enthusiasts. You will meet lots of new people, and may also be able to join an organised breeding programme to help endangered species, with members swapping and distributing fish and advice. If you do succeed in breeding your fish, keep notes as to how you did it and share the information with anyone who is interested. If it is an unusual species, you could write to an aquarists' magazine and tell them about it. The more information that is shared, the more people who will be able to join in spawning the fish.

Left: *The beautiful Arowana, revered in Japan as the Dragon Fish, is so endangered that all commerce in it is strictly regulated under CITES (Convention of International Trade in Endangered Species). For many other fish the population sizes are not known, and they may also be in urgent need of protection.*

Above: *These blackwater streams in the Amazon harbour
unique fishes, and new species are still constantly being
discovered. The same processes destroying the forest are destroying
all the smaller ecosystems found within it.*

Working for conservation

If you would like to become more involved with conservation,
there are many organisations that try to preserve all sorts of
animals and their habitats. You will be able to find one to
support that reflects your interests, such as fighting to preserve
native ponds and streams, or forests in the Amazon. You may
want to just contribute a subscription, or you could choose to
get involved in fundraising activities, or even doing practical
conservation work in the field. However little you are able to do
or contribute, it all adds up and is still worth doing.

As we watch the fish in our tanks, we are watching a little
slice of natural life that would otherwise be invisible to us. It
would be very sad if future aquarists were merely watching a
memory of something that has been lost from the world.

CHAPTER SEVEN

Treating diseases and problems

Nearly all fish diseases and ailments are avoidable. If all your fish suddenly start getting ill, it is not enough to decide which disease they have and treat it. This might work for a while, but the underlying cause will soon make them ill again and you will end up spending a fortune on disease treatments and probably become very stressed in the process. Prevention is the best remedy and fish kept in healthy conditions with a good diet are unlikely to suffer from disease.

Where do diseases come from?

Although all water, even tap water, contains some disease-causing organisms, there is nothing you can do about this. Even if you could clean the water totally, new bacteria would enter from the air and from the fish themselves. However, normally healthy fish do not usually become ill from

Opposite: *These fancy goldfish include a red/silver, white fantail, lionhead and black moor fish.*

these. Just as humans will often get a cold when they are tired and run down (even though there are not necessarily any more cold-causing organisms about than usual), so stressed and unhappy fish will be unable to fight off bacteria that normally have no effect on them. The real cure is to find out why the fish are so debilitated that they are not able to resist infection. If all the fish are affected the problem probably lies in the water, whereas if only one is prone to sickness its tank mates might be bullying it. If you buy fish that are unsuitable for your tank setup, or keep lone fish of shoaling species, those will always be stressed and prone to disease.

▌ Swimming in poison

The first thing to look at is the water. If you have been testing it regularly, and cleaning the filters, then ordinary pollution is unlikely to be a problem, but if you have been remiss about doing this, regard the first diseases as a warning sign of worse to come.

■ Sometimes poisons might enter the water from another source. If this has happened all or most of the fish in the tank will suddenly become ill, with no obvious damage. They may be hanging at the surface gasping, have turned a darker or a lighter colour than normal, or may even be trying to get out by jumping repeatedly.

■ If an irritant has entered the water the fish may try to scratch by rubbing against the tank ornaments or gravel.

■ If the room has just been painted, you have been using fly spray, or polishing the tank lid, then one of these substances may have entered

Left: *This stressed gourami is almost completely white. Abnormally dark or pale colouring is a strong indicator of stress.*

the water. Obviously it is best not to let this happen; if the room is being painted or there are other poisonous fumes, cover the tank with clingfilm and run an airline and air pump from another clean room. If you want to polish the tank hood, take it off the tank first.

Treatment: If the water has become toxic, whether it's due to an overload of fish wastes on malfunctioning filters or by the introduction of a poison, it is important to remedy the situation as soon as possible. Change fifty per cent of the water, using dechlorinated tap water of the same temperature as that in the tank. Although small water changes can be done with cold water, such a large change as this will have a big effect on the tank, and a temperature shock could be the last straw for the already upset fish. Continue doing thirty per cent water changes until the water tests show no ammonia or nitrate, and the fish are not scratching, jumping or gasping for air. This regime should take no longer than a week, and the symptoms should lessen obviously during this period. If this is not the case, then poisoning is unlikely to be the problem.

Is your filter too small?

If you set up your tank and stock it fully with baby fish, the filter will be under increasing pressure as they grow. Although you may have an aquarium that looks rather empty for a while, always take into account the full-grown size of the fish when you are stocking the tank, and allocate them enough space.

Why isn't the filter working?

The tank isn't overstocked so why has the filter stopped working? Cleaning and maintaining the filters is very important, because if they get clogged and dirty the water cannot flow through correctly and will not be filtered. Cleaning a biological filter in tap water will kill the bacteria so you should always wash sponges in old tank water. If you have to treat the fish with a medicine, make sure that the chemicals will not kill the biological filters, thereby making the problem worse. If you have accidentally damaged the bacteria in the filter, a large dose of filter starter will get the colonies thriving again.

Introducing new fish

Animals that have been exposed to disease-causing organisms often become immune to them, as their bodies develop natural defences against the known enemies. Different fish from different places, however, may have met and combated other diseases to those previously encountered by the fish in your tank. This is why the introduction of a new, seemingly healthy fish may cause an outbreak of a disease in the tank, or why the new fish may suddenly become ill as it encounters organisms that are harmless to the established inhabitants.

Some diseases may not be immediately obvious, but they may already have infected a new fish and be about to erupt. To prevent such an unpleasant surprise, ideally you should quarantine new fish in a separate tank on their own. If you do not have the facilities to do this, ask the shop if you can pay a deposit and have the fish kept for you for a month, or choose a fish from a tank that has been in the shop for a while. Sometimes this may not be possible, but keep a close watch on your tank after adding any new fish so that you can act quickly if a disease becomes apparent.

Deformations and swimming badly

Some fish are simply born damaged, or are damaged by poisons while their bodies are still growing. Obvious manifestations of this are fish that are grossly malformed on the outside, such as golden minnows with 'S' bends in their spines. Sometimes, however, it is the organs inside the fish that are deformed. Fancy goldfish have been bred to be a round shape, which is attractive to people.

Above: *The protruding eyes of this cichlid could stem from any one of a variety of causes.*

Unfortunately, this means that the swim bladder, the organ that enables the fish to keep the right way up in the water and neither bob to the top nor sink to the bottom, is unable to occupy the position and shape it would naturally. Sometimes the swim bladder is so disarranged that the fish cannot swim properly. Such fish may float, unable to swim down, or swim at a strange angle, as though their tails are lighter than their heads.

Physical deformation cannot be cured. If you see an obviously deformed fish or one swimming strangely, do not buy it. If a fish only shows swim bladder problems as it grows, these can sometimes be eased by increasing the temperature of the water or feeding a diet of mainly live foods, but the problem will always recur if you try to return the fish to a 'normal' way of life.

Sometimes deformation occurs later in life. Very old fish or fish fed on a bad diet may develop abnormalities of the spine. Also, electrical currents in the water can cause fish to develop 'bends' – a good reason for keeping your equipment in good working order (apart from the fact that faulty electrics are dangerous to you as well!). Once a deformation has occurred, it cannot be remedied. Nonetheless, many fish with slight deformations will adjust and continue to live healthy lives.

CHAPTER
SEVEN

White spot ('ick') and velvet disease

White spot is always one of the first diseases to show up on stressed fish. It is easily identified from the dusting of white spots on the body, which are cysts grown around tiny parasites. In a mild attack there

Above: *This Uaru cichlid shows the characteristic white dusting of white spot.*

may just be spots on the fins; in extreme cases the body can be completely covered. If the disease is not treated it will prove fatal, but treatment is easy and nearly always effective if given as soon as the disease starts. Velvet is a similar disease, also caused by a parasite.

Velvet disease results in a sprinkling of very fine white or yellow spots over the body, so that the fish can appear as if it has been dusted with white or gold powder.

Using medications

All medicines must be given exactly as directed in the instructions on the bottle. If you give too little, it will not kill the disease but will still stress the fish, making the problem even worse. If you give too much, it might kill the fish – most medicines are poisons, the idea being that the disease organisms will be killed by a dose that is not strong enough to kill the fish.

Always complete a course of treatment; parasites may have laid eggs, and the recommended course is designed not only to kill the adults but also the new parasites as they hatch. If you stop as soon as the fish look better, they may be re-infected.

Treatment: White spot remedies from a variety of manufacturers are available from every aquarium shop, and antiparasitic remedies are also effective against the velvet parasite. Since white spot and velvet only spend one part of their lives actually on the host fish, it is best to treat the entire tank rather than moving the sick individual. It is important to complete the course of treatment to prevent a new generation of pests attacking the fish.

▌ Fungus and 'fluffy bacteria'

A wide range of infections, caused by both bacteria and fungi, can be difficult to differentiate without microscopic examination. They show up as fluffy white or grey growths like cottonwool, and may affect the mouth, fins or body of the fish, especially where the skin or natural mucous coating of the fish has been damaged. Such damage can be caused by quarrels among the fish, incautious netting, sharp decorations or bad water conditions affecting the mucous coat. The infection will eventually eat away part of the fish and must be treated as soon as possible. Like an iceberg, the fluffy bit you can see is often only part of the problem as fungus spreads inside the fish.

▌ **Above:** *This catfish shows an outbreak of fluffy growths and reddening. Both bacteria and fungus may be present.*

> ▌ **Treatment:** Although always fatal if not dealt with, this is easy to treat. Isolate the fish if possible, and treat the water with a combined bactericide/fungicide. When the course of treatment is finished, the fish can return to its normal home.

Note: Orandas and lionhead goldfish have been specially bred to have a 'wen', a decorative growth on the head resembling a raspberry. Often the fish's natural protective mucous will gather in the pits of this growth, and may appear as fluffy growths. These are normal, and do not need treatment. Fluff on any other part of the body is abnormal and should be treated as for other fish.

CHAPTER
SEVEN

Ulcers

Ulcers also are opportunistic, often appearing where the fish has had a slight cut or knock, or attacking when bad conditions have reduced the protective mucous of the fish. At first the lesion will appear reddened, and then in later stages becomes an area of raw flesh. If it is left untreated it will extend both in area and depth, literally eating away the fish.

Above: *This gourami needs urgent attention if the ulcer is not to expand further into the body.*

Treatment: Clean healthy water is essential for successful ulcer treatment, and a bactericide from the aquarium shop may also help. In severe cases, an antibiotic, obtainable from the vet, may be necessary. Due to the large area of exposed flesh, the fish may also develop dropsy (see below).

Dropsy

Humans, who live in air, have skin to prevent body moisture escaping; without our skin we would dry up, which is why burns victims can suffer dehydration. Fish have the opposite problem. They are designed to stop the water getting in. The membranes of cells are designed to allow molecules to pass through, which is essential so that the cells can get oxygen and nutrition. However, tiny water molecules can also pass through into the cell by a process called osmosis. If this process is not limited or controlled the cell can become grossly swollen and may even burst. To stop all their cells erupting in this way, fish have skins and mucous coatings to protect them and continually pump water out of their bodies through the kidneys. Sometimes things go wrong with this system and the end result is dropsy, when the body of the fish is so swollen with water that the scales stand out from the body so that it looks like a pine cone.

Above: *This goldfish with dropsy shows the scales being lifted from the body, giving rise to the common name 'pine cone disease'.*

Dropsy is therefore a symptom, rather than a disease, and it can indicate a variety of problems. Large bare areas of flesh, such as occur in ulcers, allow water to enter. The kidneys of the sick fish must therefore work overtime to expel it, putting even more of a load on the constitution of a fish that is already ill. Bacterial or viral infections, or even just being 'under the weather', may hamper the workings of the kidneys, so that normal water intake is not excreted properly.

Water has a different 'osmotic pressure' depending on its composition and the amount of substances dissolved in it. Sea water, with lots of salt dissolved in it, has a lower osmotic pressure than fresh, and less water will pass into cells through their membranes. Each species of fish has evolved to cope with the osmotic pressure of the type of water in which it naturally lives, so marine fish placed in fresh water will die as a result of the extra osmotic pressure.

Marine and fresh waters are an extreme example, but the same stresses occur to a lesser extent when softwater fish are kept in hard water and vice versa. Some fish can cope with a

Right: *This catfish is so bloated with the retained liquid of dropsy that it will be unable to move properly.*

CHAPTER
SEVEN

Using more than one medication

If the disease you are trying to treat may be caused by one of several different infections, you may need to use more than one medicine. Never give two treatments simultaneously; the chemicals may react, rendering the treatment ineffective or possibly lethal. If two treatments are necessary, complete one course, wait a week to let the fish recover and to see if there is any improvement, and then try the next if necessary.

greater range of osmotic pressures than others, but if the water is too different they can't regulate their water content and will either dehydrate (freshwater fish in salt water) or they may become overloaded with water (saltwater fish in fresh water). Keeping a fish in water towards the edges of its tolerance may not kill it immediately, but the strain of keeping its body regulated may leave it prone to disease.

Treatment: Since salt water has a lower osmotic pressure than fresh, sometimes keeping a fish with dropsy in a slight salt solution will decrease the water entering the body. This will give the fish's organs time to recover without the strain of trying to expel all the extra water so that it will be able to resume normal functioning when it returns to normal water. All changes should be made slowly. The fish should be isolated and 7.5 ml (½ tablespoon) of salt per 4.8 litres (8 pints) added over a period of time. As the fish recovers, use water changes to dilute the salt solution until the water is back to normal.

If the cause is bacterial, antibiotics from the vet may help. Some people suggest drawing off body fluids with a hypodermic syringe, but such a procedure is likely to do more harm than good and should not be attempted.

Popeye

Properly known as exophthalmia, this is caused by a buildup of fluid behind the eye, which makes the eye bulge outwards. It can be caused by eye flukes (a parasite), bacterial infections and bad water quality, being a symptom rather than a disease in itself.

Treatment: Initially bad water quality may be suspected, but if this is not the case bactericide treatments may be effective, as can be an anti-parasite remedy.

Growths

Growths on fish may have a variety of causes. Smooth lumps that appear to be pushing up the skin rather than on it may be the first sign of an ulcer starting or may be a cancerous tumour. Round yellow or white nodules on the skin may be cancers or the result of parasite infestations – each growth may contain thousands of parasites. Either of these possibilities cannot be practically treated, and the priority in the latter case must be to avoid infection of the other aquarium inhabitants.

Growths that afflict the skin include the waxy carp pox and the rough nodules of lymphocystis, particularly on fins or at the site of a wound. Both of these are untreatable, being caused by viruses. Fish may recover of their own accord, but will continue to carry the virus and may infect other fishes.

Right: *Tumours, can sometimes be removed by surgery if they are accessible.*

INDEX